RIGHT PLACE, RIGHT TIME

Sidney, Heather, Boomer and Me

RIGHT PLACE, RIGHT TIME
Sidney, Heather, Boomer and Me

Bruce Rainnie

Forewords by Heather Moyse and Scott Russell

The Acorn Press
Charlottetown
2012

P.O. Box 22024
Charlottetown, Prince Edward Island
C1A 9J2
acornpresscanada.com

Design and layout by Matt Reid

Cover photo by Alanna Jankov

Printed and Bound in Canada by Friesen's

Library and Archives Canada Cataloguing in Publication

Rainnie, Bruce, 1967-
    Right place, right time : Sidney, Heather, Boomer and me / Bruce Rainnie.

ISBN 978-1-894838-70-2

    1. Rainnie, Bruce, 1967-. 2. Broadcasters--Prince Edward Island--Biography. 3. Broadcasters--Canada--Biography. 4. Sportscasters-- Canada--Biography. I. Title.

PN1992.4.R33A3 2012   384.54092   C2012-901102-9

 Canada Council **Conseil des Arts** for the Arts **du Canada**

The publisher acknowledges the support of the Government of Canada through the Canada Book Fund of the Department of Canadian Heritage, the Canada Council for the Arts Block Grant Program and the support of the Province of Prince Edward Island.

To Mark and Alistair, my main little men...

When I was a boy, I thought my Dad was the tallest man in the world. On many days, I still do. I hope you guys think your Dad is tall for a long time, too.

Contents

Foreword

My first up-close, in-person experience with PEI's CBC anchor, Bruce Rainnie – probably the most recognized person on Prince Edward Island (along with his weatherman, Boomer Gallant) – came over the 2005 Christmas holidays. I had just qualified to compete in the upcoming Olympic Winter Games in Torino in February 2006 in the women's bobsleigh event. The kicker was that my first time sliding down a bobsleigh track had been October 11, 2005 – only two-and-a-half months before.

Bruce contacted me to do an on-camera special feature interview while I was home, as I'm sure he had lots of questions to ask. The camera crew filmed me doing part of my workout at the gym, and then they came to my parents' home for the interview. I think what surprised Bruce more than my very quick Olympic qualification was that he only had to ask me three questions before we (I) took up the whole film! Bruce still teases me to this day about my "verbosity."

Bruce and I have become very good friends over the past five years, and he never ceases to amaze me with his stories. It's not only that he has so many astounding experiences and encounters from which he can draw, but that he has a marvelous storytelling ability with an incredibly uncanny memory for detail. You will actually be able to see the twinkle in his eye and hear the excitement and occasional irony in his voice as you read through the lines and pages of this entertaining book.

Bruce recounts stories and hilarious adventures that he and Boomer have shared throughout their years together, both on and off camera, and gives us some epic comedic moments from live interviews with Fred "The Fiddler" MacDonald. For those of you who have watched Fiddler and Boomer in action, these written segments will have you reminiscing and laughing out loud as you read. And for those of you who have never seen or met either one of them, Bruce does such a wonderful job at recounting these infamous Boomer moments and "Fiddler'isms" that you, too, will be hard-pressed to keep the laughter in.

Although he wasn't born on PEI, Bruce is as proud an Islander as they come. And we are extremely lucky to have him here with us. He is a remarkably caring person and down-to-earth, and he has earned the respect of some of the most notable and recognized people in the world. He is engaging and utterly hilarious, and will make you smile, if not laugh out loud (which I suspect you will), while he introduces you to his world. Islanders continue to tune in to CBC News to watch their favourite anchor tell them what's going on in the world, on the Island, and with interesting individuals. So here's your opportunity to see the behind-the-scenes Bruce – embarrassing moments, bloopers, personal thoughts, and some of his Top Ten lists.

Blessed with the ability to make us laugh and enrich the world around him with his unique and generous gifts, Bruce has entered people's homes via the evening news, and has entered their hearts through the grace of his genuine nature and his witty sense of humour. Not only is this a great read and a good addition to your personal library, but in buying this book you will also be contributing to a great cause, as every penny from the proceeds of its sale is being donated to cancer research (in memory of Boomer's late wife, Mae). So sit back, relax, and enjoy the privilege of going behind the scenes with PEI's biggest celebrity, as well as the abdominal workout you will get from laughing at some of his experiences!

Smiles...

Heather Moyse
2010 Olympic Gold Medalist
Motivational & Keynote Speaker
Proud Prince Edward Islander

Bonus Foreword

The thing about Prince Edward Island is that it gets into your blood. Although you arrive with few connections, inevitably there are links made that manage to last a lifetime.

When I was still quite young, my parents took our family to "The Island" on a summer vacation. One star-filled evening we watched with amazement on a black-and-white TV in a small motel near Summerside as the first man walked on the moon.

It was an experience that shaped a way of considering the world and an important part of life yet to come. "There are endless horizons now," my father remarked at the time. "This is a special moment."

Years later, as a graduate of the Journalism School at the University of Western Ontario, I was considering my first real posting as a broadcaster. I had won a spot as a summer intern at CBC and, with the exception of my native Toronto, had the choice to work at any station in the country.

"Choose PEI," my father told me. "Remember, horizons are endless there. For you it will be a special place."

He was never more right.

In Charlottetown, and across the province, I encountered the people and things that became the building blocks of my outlook. From the mystical standard bred horses that patrolled the Charlottetown Driving Park and the wonder of the Gold Cup and Saucer to the immense beauty of the dunes and ocean shore, I was filled with a sense of comfort. With the kindnesses of so many people, the place began to feel safe very quickly and a lingering homesickness for the big city melted away.

I met my wife, Catherine, in Charlottetown when she came to be a radio producer at CBC. Together we discovered so much love and happiness in the community. When we moved away to Montreal it was with substantial heartache and more than a tinge of regret.

Bruce has captured this joyous feeling in his reminiscences and anecdotes, which form the basis of this remarkable book. The characters come to life under his witty and discerning glare. Boomer, Heather, and Sidney are the headliners – but there are so many others delivered to us as treasures of his charmed life.

Like Bruce, I've been able to experience the world and all of the glorious things that go along with this privileged position that we've both somehow lucked into. I've traveled the globe many times over and been to the Olympic Games. I've met the "World's Fastest Man," seen the colossus that is China, and the exact spot off the coast of South Africa where the Indian and Atlantic Oceans converge.

But, like Bruce, I still maintain a greater appreciation for the things that are closer to the heart...closer to home.

Before the 2010 Olympics I was in Prince Edward Island at Bruce's request to speak at a community dinner in honour of Heather Moyse, who was yet to become the gold medalist at the Vancouver/Whistler Games. It was one of the most moving experiences of my life.

To understand the reverence that the people of this place can have for one of their children who has made them proud is simply awe-inspiring. It's the kind of thing that happens with regularity on PEI because people like Bruce never fail to remind us of an abundance of greatness that lives right next door.

I only met Mae Gallant a handful of times but recall her grace and understated generosity. To know that this book honours her memory and continues the good work of the PEI Cancer Treatment Centre is comforting.

One of the most prized possessions I can claim was given to me on the day I moved away from PEI. It's a framed "Order in Council" signed by Gerard Mitchell, a Justice of the Supreme Court of Prince Edward Island, and it bears the official seal of the province. It legally adopts me as a "Prince Edward Islander."

"I order that henceforward wherever else he may be or go from time to time," wrote Justice Mitchell, "that he may refer to himself by the appellation 'Islander' or as being from 'The Island' or by any other variation of these terms that are sometimes used by the people of Prince Edward Island to refer to their beloved homeland."

Bruce goes one step further. He lovingly reflects on his adopted home in every word that he writes in this rollicking story of so many blessed characters.

He demonstrates once again what many of us have known all along. Prince Edward Island is a magical place of endless horizons.

Scott Russell
CBC Sports

Preface

A very wise man and I were once discussing an age-old phenomenon: how ten different people could all witness the exact same event and then, days later, have ten widely varying versions of what happened. "Maybe, just maybe," the wise man surmised, "this proves that recollection is just the manipulation of memory."

In other words, there is what is actually seen and heard, and then there is what's remembered. The difference between the two quite often offers a lesson in history and imagination, because the human impulse is always to perfect the former with the latter.

So there you have it – my long-winded way of admitting that most of what you're about to read is true, but not all of it. After all, how could it be, given that many of the stories you're about to read relate to conversations or events that happened decades ago. So, I freely admit up front that in the pages that follow, I will be prone to the rare embellishment. But I will also strictly adhere to a principle first advanced by the comedian George Burns: "If you're going to lie, make it sound as much like the truth as possible, make it funny, and make sure no one gets hurt!"

Here is how this project came to be. December of 2011 marked a couple of significant, though disparate, milestones in my life – the 25th year of being paid to work as a broadcaster, and the 5th anniversary of the death of Boomer Gallant's wife, Mae. This book is the result of reflecting on each. Many amazing, hilarious, poignant, and priceless things have happened to me in the last quarter-century when my microphone has been in the "on" position. I'd like to share some of these memories with you. I also want to appropriately pay tribute to a wonderful friend, so, with the help of countless people, I have, I hope, found a way. I'm so pleased to tell you that every cent made from the sale of this book will be directed to the PEI Cancer Treatment Centre in memory of Mae Gallant. With your help, I hope we make a bundle.

This book isn't a novel per se, nor does it strictly adhere to any sort of chronology. Rather, it's a series of loosely connected riffs and lists and stories that, ideally, you can pick up and put down at any time.

That being said, you will notice quite quickly that three characters appear a lot. What follows in the pages ahead is primarily about my relationship with my weatherman, Boomer Gallant, and secondarily about my interactions with two Olympic Gold medalists, Sidney Crosby and Heather Moyse.

I've known Sidney since he was ten years old, and I was the reporter for the first television story ever done on the young hockey sensation. To say I'm proud of that would be a colossal understatement. Even as a kid, Sidney's maturity and politeness were off the charts. As a young man, they remain there. That's a testament to his parents, Trina and Troy, and to the inherent decency of Sidney himself.

I first met Heather Moyse during the run-up to the 2006 Winter Olympics in Torino, Italy. I was dazzled at first sight by her total lack of pretension and obvious devotion to home. My admiration for her has only grown as the years have passed. I've said this before and I'll repeat it here: if you're a parent and are looking to steer your child toward a role model, you don't have to look any further than Heather Moyse.

Which brings us to Kevin "Boomer" Gallant. I can't go anywhere on PEI without someone asking me, "Where's Boomer?" The fact that we are seen as a team and inseparable is very cool, and something I cultivate and cherish.

When I had the opportunity in 2003 to apply to host the Compass program, one of the primary factors that swayed me to do so was the chance to work with Boomer. I just had a sense it would be special. What I didn't know was that it would evolve into a once-in-a-lifetime partnership.

Boomer is my dream on-air foil. I get asked all the time, "Do you ever rehearse what you're going to say to each other?" The answer is an emphatic, "No!" I know I can say anything to him and something clever or funny will come back. I think he knows the same. The result is a relationship that might be unique on North American television.

Behind all the teasing and poking and prodding you see on-air, though, there is a deep respect and unbreakable bond between two guys who would do anything for each other. The rarest person in life is someone who's not just a friend to your face, but also a friend behind your back. He's that guy for me, and I hope I'm that guy for him.

Which is not to say that we don't thoroughly enjoy abusing one another. And that brings us full-circle to the point I tried to make at the top of this introduction: tall tales are an essential part of the Bruce-Boomer relationship, and some, admittedly, are about to grow stilts in the retelling.

By the way, the wise man (probably the wisest I've ever met) is Dr. Wade Kenny. Wade is presently a professor at Mount St. Vincent University in Halifax. But back in 1983, He was my grade 10 English teacher at Dartmouth High School. Apart from my Mom and Dad, he is without doubt the person who most influenced me in those formative, teenage years. He taught me to play the guitar, introduced me to Ernest Hemingway and Paul Simon, helped me dissect and understand *Julius Caesar* – my favourite Shakespeare play – encouraged an interest in public speaking, and helped me foster what has become a lifelong love of reading and writing. I owe him a belated and heartfelt thanks.

I hope he enjoys this book and I hope you do, too.

Acknowledgements

To Terrilee Bulger at The Acorn Press for believing in this project from the very instant she heard about it.

To my editor, Ann Thurlow. When I started this book, I very quickly became fanatical about making sure it was in my voice, that the words sounded as they were coming from me and only me. Ann sensed this early on, and geared her entire editing process toward me achieving this goal. And during those times when the well was starting to dry up a bit, she was very skilful with her subtle nudges.

To Matt Reid. What a designer! You have a wonderful gift - the ability to make all worries about fonts, colours, and layout totally disappear.

To Alanna Jankov. Thank you for sharing your keen eye, and for donating your gifts and time to this effort.

To Wade Kenny and Jim Falcone. I went to Dartmouth High while the two of you were English teachers there. Best timing ever...

To Lou LeBlanc. Thanks for setting me on a path I've loved. I've never forgotten your generosity. Still trying to get down that tree, though!

To the staff at Radio CJLS in Yarmouth, in particular Grant Wyman for never tightening the reins as much as he could have; Ray Zinck for showing me what professional work ethic and storytelling should be; and Dave Hall for fostering a mood where mistakes weren't disasters and where creativity could thrive.

To the staff at CBC PEI, but especially producer Tracy Lightfoot. Tracy has sat through multiple retellings of virtually every story in this book. About a year ago, her exact words were, "You know, you've had a charmed life – you should write some of these things down before you forget them." As usual, her advice was spot-on.

To all who work behind the scenes for CBC Sports, but especially producers Jeff Pearlman and Don Peppin, retired producers Donna Warner and Joe Recupero, and director Chris Elias. Your unwavering belief has allowed me to see and talk about things I once could only dream about.

To Scott Russell. You're simply the best at what you do. It's a pleasure and inspiration to watch you work.

To Alex J. Walling. In 1995, you walked by me in the press box at the Halifax Metro Centre, stopped, turned around, and said to me, "You're the new guy on CBC, aren't you? You're raw, but there's potential." You were right, and I've enjoyed every conversation since.

To Maritime broadcasting legend Pat Connolly. You showed in your work that it was possible to be analytical without being boring, and critical without being a jerk. I'm glad you've always been there for me to look up to.

To Bill Robinson and the staff at the Nova Scotia Sport Hall of Fame. Our relationship goes back fifteen years now. I hope the years to come are just as memorable.

To Dr. Roland Muise, John MacIntosh, Al MacLean, Mickey Fox, Peter Halpin, and the late Sandy Bain. Your best friends know when to give you a pat on the back, and know when to give you a kick in the pants. These guys have been there for multiple pats and kicks.

To the people of Prince Edward Island. Thanks for so warmly embracing a CFA (come from away). You've always made me and my family feel so much at home. Nobody crowds you here, but nobody goes it alone either. Can't ask for much more than that...

To Brenda, Mark, and Matthew Rainnie. I would never have been in any right place at any right time without you. Enough said...

To Sidney, Heather, and Boomer. I am eternally grateful that I was in the right place at the right time to establish life-long friendships with each of you...

To Kendra. Our journey feels like it's just begun. If I could go back in time and do it all again with you, I wouldn't change a single thing.

MAE GALLANT

Mae Gallant never had a bad thing to say about anybody. It sounds like a glib assertion, one too good to be true, because even the kindest of souls is prone to the occasional negative utterance. But not Mae Gallant. Not once – ever.

This is not to suggest for a moment, however, that she didn't relish the opportunity to get the last word in, especially when her husband, Boomer, was on the receiving end.

I remember a Sunday night in 2005 as though it was yesterday. Boomer and I were "rehearsing" for a "performance" we were giving the next evening in support of the Charlottetown Food Bank. Mae was there, and so was my wife, Kendra.

I recall vividly Mae sinking back into a La-Z-Boy chair, a look equal parts amusement and resignation creasing her eternally pleasant face. Boomer had just left the room with his garbage bag full of costumes when Mae looked skyward, shook her head, smiled softly, and said aloud, "My husband is the only man I know who has to decide which of his TWO Elvis suits he is going to wear!"

Sure enough, it was a big decision. On one hand, there was the "Aloha from Hawaii" suit, complete with jewel-studded cape. A beauty, really. On the other hand, a sensational white vinyl number with tassels on the arms and pants that flared wildly at the ankles. This was my personal favourite, because it came with instructions that suggested the costume wearer should not stand too close to an open flame.

The vinyl suit was tried first, and, despite my best attempts to steer Boomer near a couple of Christmas candles, he left the room unscathed. When he descended the stairs minutes later in the

"Aloha" ensemble, though, he brought all conversation in the room to a complete standstill. Uncomfortable silence enveloped the room. And here's why...

The top of the costume looked fine, but the pants were among the most ill-fitting in the history of men's clothing. To be more precise, they were egregiously unyielding in the crotch area.

Yes, indeed, before our very eyes, Elvis had been joined by two tiny little Rolling Stones.

Looking in that general area, I wondered if we were in for six more weeks of winter: the resemblance to Wiarton Willie was that extreme.

Boomer stood there for what was likely seconds, but seemed like excruciating minutes, when Mae finally did what she had to do – break the silence.

"Boom," she said. "I don't think you should wear that one."

"Why, dear?" he replied.

She paused, took a deep breath, and, with timing worthy of Johnny Carson, David Letterman, or Don Rickles, said...

"Don't you think the Island knows enough of your shortcomings already?"

It just doesn't get any better than that.

Mae Gallant passed away in December of 2006 after a spirited battle with liver cancer. There's not a day that goes by we don't think of her. I hope that never changes.

Mae, this one's for you.

THE BROADCASTING BUG

"Find a job you love, and you'll never work a day in your life."
– Old Irish Proverb

My Mom and I used to have a ritual. Every year from kindergarten to grade 9, on the very last day of school, she would sit me down and ask me what I wanted to be when I grew up. I'd make my choice and then tear outside to throw or hit some kind of ball. She'd then record my answer on the appropriate page in my School Days Treasure Album.

Looking back, the responses are at times predictable and at times preposterous – policeman, pilot, church minister (stop laughing, Boomer), doctor, accountant, and professional basketball player (a realistic goal – after all, what NBA team doesn't hunger for a slow six-foot guy who can't jump?).

Never once was the choice broadcaster. I can honestly tell you that in those years, the thought never even entered my head. But it should have, especially had I been paying closer attention to the evolving evidence. Consider the following...

1) At the age of three, I called my first imaginary hockey game into my parents' "new" reel-to-reel tape recorder (yes, a machine that actually predated cassettes). One of my earliest childhood memories is of sitting there with the tiny microphone in my equally tiny hand, waiting for my Dad to say, "Go!" What a thrill it was! This technology was so cutting-edge for the time, and for a toddler it was utterly mind-blowing. My parents still have the machine, by the way, and they still have my first "broadcast." Once every five years or so, my Dad will dig it all out, set it all up, and press

"play." What follows is a riveting account of a spectacular (and quite economical) passing play between three Montreal Canadiens forwards.

"Mo-hov-o-leetch got it, he passes to Reesh-ard,
Reesh-ard got it now, he passes to Corn-why-ayy,
Corn-why-ayy got it now, he skates, and he still got it,
He shoots, he scooooreeeesss!!!"

You have to ask yourself – has a hockey announcer of any age ever been more attached to the past tense of the verb "get?" I don't think so.

2) As I watched sports on television at an early age, not only could I name the players on every team, I could also name for you the announcers who broadcast that team's games. For instance, I could tell you that Danny Gallivan and Dick Irvin were the voices of the Montreal Canadiens, that Bill Hewitt and Brian McFarlane were the same for the Toronto Maple Leafs, and that Dick Stockton and Ken Harrelson were in the booth for the Boston Red Sox. The way these men used their voices to help create excitement, the command they had of the English language, their use of colourful verbs – all of this transfixed me just as much as the action taking place on the ice or diamond.

3) At each level of schooling (elementary, junior high, senior high), I relished every chance to speak publicly, either in front of the class or in front of the entire student body. Admittedly, verbal presentations always made me nervous, but it was always more of an invigorating-nervous as opposed to a paralyzing-nervous. It consistently shocked me to discover that the majority of my classmates were wired exactly opposite.

4) Midway through my grade 12 year, I made a pitch to Dartmouth Community Cable Television to produce and host my own weekly television program. At that time, there was no local programming geared toward youth, and the program director thought I could help fill a void. What followed was the eponymously titled "Rainnie

and Friends." It was loosely modeled on Johnny Carson's Tonight Show – I had a desk, a sidekick, and would kiss female guests on the hand when they approached the set ('cause Johnny did). This show aired every Saturday night for two years on channel 10 in Dartmouth and developed a bit of a cult following. (Okay, that might be overstating it a bit, but I do recall once being recognized at the Kentucky Fried Chicken on Wyse Road.) It was also easily the worst thing to ever grace airwaves anywhere on this planet we call "Earth." Seriously, if you think of the most atrocious thing you've ever seen on television and double it, you're still not even in the ballpark of "Rainnie and Friends." Thank goodness all video records of this abomination are on Beta tape, and that Beta players are tougher to find than an accurate Boomer Gallant weather forecast. As awful as it was, though, I can tell you this: I just loved doing it, and at the time was proud of the finished product almost each and every week.

So, given all of the above, it's quite clear I've always had a passion for and been fascinated by broadcasting. Still, though, I never even remotely thought of it as a career. Not once. That is, until Rick Hansen decided to wheel his chair around the world back in the mid-1980s. Now, if that statement seems harder to follow than a Fiddler MacDonald train of thought, I understand. It certainly deserves further explanation...

Rick Hansen's Man in Motion tour began with little fanfare in March of 1985. By September of 1986, though, he was a worldwide phenomenon and the tour had gained huge momentum. So, it was big news when it was announced that, on his long trek home to Vancouver, he would stop for a visit in Dartmouth, Nova Scotia.

At that time, the Events Coordinator for the City of Dartmouth was a very talented and creative woman by the name of Linda Hall (she has since become Linda Gourlay, and for the past decade has been the editor of *Saltscapes Magazine*). Linda was charged with organizing a massive waterfront reception for Mr. Hansen on the day he arrived in the city. One thing she wanted above almost anything else was for a song to be written and performed for the occasion. And here's where fate had a bit of fun...

Through some common acquaintances, I knew Linda a little. And she knew me enough to be aware that I played guitar and dabbled a bit in song-writing. Now, this is not to say that there weren't at least a thousand better guitar players and songwriters in the city. There definitely were. I just happened to be in her line of sight at just the right time. See what I mean about "Right place, right time?"

So, on September 19 of 1986, I stepped onto a makeshift stage on the Dartmouth waterfront, sporting my best brown tweed blazer (the one with the patches on the elbows), my hair parted in the middle and feathered back on the sides. Straight ahead of me was a sea of 12,000 faces. To my immediate left was Rick Hansen. Hesitantly finger-picking a D-chord, I waited excruciating seconds for my knees to stop shaking, and then launched straight into verse one of "A Hero's Song."

> The road is dark, his arms grow tired,
> Still six more miles tonight.
> The challenge grows, so on he goes,
> Committed to his fight.

> His outlook has never once grown dim,
> When his strength has been unsure,
> His heart has never once said, "Stop,"
> When his mind has said, "No more."

In the interest of time, I'll spare you the rest of this masterpiece. I can tell you that when it was over, the crowd actually clapped (a huge relief) and Rick Hansen politely whispered, "Thanks, I really liked that."* (He, like me, must have been a sucker for songs with three chords and the a-b-c-b rhyme scheme.)

And that was it, or so I thought. The very next day, however, I received a call from CHNS radio in Halifax, asking if I could drop by their studio to talk a bit about the experience of playing this song in front of Rick Hansen. I appeared on a show called Maritime Morning, which was co-hosted by Elizabeth Logan and Lou LeBlanc. I guess it went well because after we were finished, Lou took me aside and told me how much he enjoyed the interview. He also asked me if I had ever thought about broadcasting as a career. When I told him I hadn't, he suggested we get together for lunch the next day to talk some more.

I've always been touched that an established professional took such an interest in the future of a nineteen-year-old kid. Lou and I talked that day for what must have been two hours. I remember so much of what he told me, but nothing stands out so much as his response to my question, "So, what separates the good broadcasters from those who are truly great?"

His answer: "The best broadcasters in the world can talk themselves up a tree to the very highest branch, get totally stuck, and then smoothly talk their way back down – all without anyone in the audience ever knowing they were in any sort of trouble."

Those words were like an epiphany to me. The moment he said them, I was totally hooked. Any job that offered such a mixture of adventure, challenge, uncertainty, and fulfillment – it was something I just had to pursue. Within a week, Lou had arranged work for me as a part-time announcer at CHNS, and my life of verbally climbing tree branches had begun.

That was twenty-five years ago, and, to be truthful, I'm not sure I've ever discovered the smoothest way to get down. The right path can be so darn elusive! But even if I never find it, that's okay – life at the top of the tree, even on the most daunting of days, still beats working for a living.

———

*It turns out Rick Hansen really did like the tune, and so, apparently, did his handlers. Moments after the ceremony concluded, a member of the Hansen team approached me and asked if my song could be used in an upcoming National Film Board documentary on the Man in Motion tour. I could not have agreed more readily, although a voice in the back of my head wondered if the guy was just being nice. That nagging voice was silenced some six months later, when I received a formal invitation to attend a premiere of the Hansen documentary at the Oxford Theatre in Halifax. Knowing that my song would be prominently featured, I invited an extensive group of family and friends to attend with me. As the film began, I sat there with nervous anticipation, anxious to see where the filmmakers would choose to use my words and melody. Maybe it would accompany a montage of Hansen pushing his chair commandingly against a sunlit sky. Or maybe it would provide a subtle backdrop to a sequence where the sun dips on the horizon as Hansen tries to squeeze in one last daylight mile. With expectation at a crescendo, I sat there with my ample group, and waited...and waited...and waited some more. Nothing. No sign of the song whatsoever. And then, like an arrow through my heart, the credits started to roll. Everyone in our row sat stone silent. The credits continued. No one would make any sort of eye contact with me. The credits continued. I sat there, comatose. Finally, at the 89-minute, 50-second mark of this 90-minute film, when the "gaffer" and "key grip" were being identified on the huge screen in front of us, the chorus of the song began – and continued for 9 whole seconds before fading out. And that was it. I believe it was my brother who captured the mood perfectly when he said, "Well, you have to look on the bright side – at least they got it in before the lights came up in the theatre!"

BOOMER: THE SCHOOL VISIT

The CBC Compass program is an amazing part of the culture and upbringing here on PEI, and nothing drives that home more than being recognized by school-aged children. I can guarantee that you could go to any other province in Canada and most elementary school students would have a tough time naming the personalities on their provincial supper-hour news show. Young kids and news programs generally don't mix. But they sure do on PEI! Parents start their kids early on Compass, and the result is interesting. Not only can the youth of PEI typically name Bruce and Boomer, I hazard to say that they actually think we're kind of cool. Not totally cool, mind you, but kind of.

One of the offshoots of this is that Boomer and I receive several requests a year to visit Island schools. We can't honour them all, but we do try to get in as many as possible. Because of schedules, however, it's very rare that we're able to be at the same school at the same time. When this does happen, though, it's always memorable, at least for me. Which leads us to this story...

Late during the fierce winter of 2011, Boomer was invited by a Charlottetown elementary school to talk to the grade 2 students about weather (his alleged specialty). He knew I had a free morning, so he suggested I tag along. When I agreed, little did I realize that what was about to ensue would be a four-pronged attack on my comedic senses, one that still reverberates to this day. Let me take you back...

Boomer and I arrived and were greeted ever so sweetly and warmly by a group of about thirty seven-year-olds. Boomer, in particular, was in his element – he stood peacock-like at the head of the class, dressed as usual in his three-tone Hawaiian shirt, faded Boston Red Sox cap, and weather-defying, bunion-revealing, open-toed sandals. Oozing confidence and fully in command, he opened up the floor to questions.

Now generally in a setting like this, what would follow would be of this variety:

"Why do you like your job?"

"Why is the sky blue?"

"When is the snow going to stop?"

"Is this the worst winter ever?"

Good questions all, but the students at this school had done their homework, and wanted to take Boomer just a wee bit deeper. As I sat in the corner, content to watch this meteorological master at work, a little boy we'll call "Andrew" put up his hand to kick off the proceedings:

"Boomer, how do tornadoes form?"

Boomer shifted a bit awkwardly from one foot to another, clearly not anticipating so profound a query. After a moment to collect his thoughts, he responded:

"Good question, Andrew, very good question. Boy, those tornadoes, they're pretty amazing, aren't they? We've never had one here on PEI, and I sure hope we never do."

"Yeah, but how do they form?"

"You know, they're a bit like water spouts, but water spouts tend to dissipate when they get over land."

"Yes, but how do they form?"

"I'll tell ya, some of those tornadoes are strong enough to pick up houses and cows. If I ever see one, I'm going to drive away as fast as I can! I mean, I'll be going really fast!"

"That's nice, but how do they form?"

"Thank you, Andrew. Let's see if anyone else has a question."

At this point, I can no longer make eye contact with Boomer. My strategy is to stare at the ground so nobody will see me shaking.

Little Sally's hand goes into the air, and Round 2 commences...

"Boomer, my grandfather lives in the country, and there seems like there's less snow in his field than there is on lawns here in the city. Why is that?"

(Remember the perplexed look Joe Clark used to get on his face when he tried to answer questions in French? Same look now on Boomer's face...)

"Excellent question, Sally. What happens in the country is that the fields are open with no trees around, and the snow is able to blow around and not build up."

(Hey – so far a good answer, something to build on...)

"But in the city what happens is that the snow hits things like houses or cars or buildings, and piles start to form."

(Really an excellent response, had he stopped there. But he didn't. Thrusting his fingers upward to form air quotes and accentuate his next big word, he continued.)

"We in the weather business call that 'FRICTION.' Yes, that's right, we call it 'FRICTION.'"

(At this point, I turn away and face the chalkboard.)

(Since that day, by the way, whenever I want to win any argument with Boomer, I simply form air quotes and scream, "FRICTION." Never fails to elicit a colourful response.)

A question from Samuel initiates a truly fateful Round 3...

"Boomer, is the moon bouncy?"

A bit spooked, Boomer hesitantly responds, "Now, why do you ask that, Samuel?"

"Because when you see movies of astronauts walking on the moon, they bounce up and down."

"Well, Samuel, there's a simple reason for that. You see, the gravity on the moon is so strong that when the astronauts jump up, it pushes them back down!"

(At this point, the kids look puzzled and the teachers look concerned.)

"But I thought there was no gravity on the moon."

I am convulsing in the corner when Boomer plaintively looks to me and says, "Bruce, you take this one!"

Emily is next with a question that, under most conditions, would be innocent enough:

"Boomer, what do you do when you wake up in the morning?"

Boomer has been through the wringer by this point, and is clearly feeling the need to save the day with a big, big finish. He takes a deep breath, steadies himself, and responds...

"What do I do first thing in the morning? Well, usually, I get up and STRETCH! That's right, I stretch."

(Somebody please send some paramedics to the corner of the classroom – I'm toast!)

I've known Boomer extremely well for almost a decade now, and I can tell you that the only times I've ever seen him stretch were when the TV remote or his Alpine were out of reach. I assure you, this is not a man waking up in the morning and immediately engaging in calisthenics.

So, all in all: a day I'll never forget. I'm also strongly committed to making sure Boomer doesn't forget it either. And I am forever indebted to the wonderful group of grade 2 students who turned a routine school visit into an exhausting trial by fire for my beloved weatherman.

STARTING IN YARMOUTH

After a thorough tour of the radio station and the chance to meet most of the staff, the moment of truth had arrived.

I was in the office of the program director. He was seated behind his desk as I nervously shifted in a chair across from him. Summoning every ounce of courage I could muster, I somehow forced the following from my mouth:

"So, how much does the job pay?"

"Fifteen thousand," he said, not missing a beat.

Not quite believing what I had heard, I pressed onward.

"Is that for the full year, or just for the first six months?"

Smiling, he replied, "That's the yearly salary. But I'll tell you what – if your first three months go well, we'll bump that up a bit."

Heartened by this potentiality, I decided to probe deeper...

"By how much, do you think?"

"Well, if you really impress us, we could go as high as fifteen-five."

And with that assurance, I accepted my first-ever, full-time, professional broadcasting job. At age twenty-one, I was the morning show announcer at Radio CJLS in Yarmouth, Nova Scotia.

I studied chemistry at Dalhousie University and always had aspirations to one day become an orthopaedic surgeon. This was before I was bitten so forcefully by the broadcasting bug. I can't begin to describe the silence that enveloped the dinner table the night I broke the news to my parents that I was planning to suspend my studies and go work for a radio station. Put yourself in their shoes – after years of thinking their eldest son would become a doctor, they instead learn he's about to head to Yarmouth to become a DJ. I remember assuring them that I would give it my best shot and try to move quickly up the broadcast ladder. I further assured them that if it didn't work out, I would continue my studies. To their credit, they took me totally at my word and, after the initial shock wore off, supported my decision in every possible way.*

This was April of 1989. I thought I might spend a year in Yarmouth, maybe two at the most. What I underestimated was how much I'd love the town, my colleagues, and the job. I wound up working there for 5½ wonderful years and found it to be the most valuable experience a young announcer could ever have. Why? Well, in addition to hosting the morning show, I had the chance to do virtually everything else, too – prepare and present newscasts, prepare and present weather forecasts, develop and deliver sportscasts, write and voice commercials, host remote broadcasts, read funeral announcements, host fundraising radio-thons – the list goes on. But by far the most educational of all my CJLS endeavours had its origins in a conversation I had one day in 1994 with the station manager, Grant Wyman.

"How would you like a new challenge?" he asked.

"Sure," I eagerly answered.

"In addition to your morning show, I'd like you to host a 60-minute, noon-hour, information-entertainment program. We'll do it every weekday and call it 'Rainnie at Noon.'"

Without having any idea of the work this would entail, I blurted something clever like, "Bring it on!"

"Rainnie at Noon" ran for the next two years, until I left CJLS for the CBC. It taught me so much about the challenges of producing and hosting a daily one-hour program. For one thing – what do you do when a guest doesn't show up? This happened with alarming regularity. I remember one time in particular I had booked Miss D'Entremont from the West Pubnico Garden Club. She was going to spend a riveting hour talking about her various planting strategies. And then, at about ten minutes to noon, she called to tell me that Claude, the man she'd been eyeing up for more than year, had finally phoned to ask her to lunch. Suffice to say, she wasn't about to turn down Claude. So, there I was, an hour to fill and no one to talk about begonias or hollyhocks. Events like this either break you or build your foundation as a broadcaster. In my case, they taught me very quickly to think on my feet and find creative ways to fill time. Impromptu games of trivia with the audience were a favourite. Suggesting a controversial topic and opening the phone lines was also an occasionally successful fallback. More often than not, though, it came down to talking about the details of my day and trying to make them sound mildly interesting. Remember Lou LeBlanc's tree? Man, was I stuck up there a lot!

It was also in Yarmouth that I began to fully understand and appreciate the art of conducting an interview. They say you learn the most from your mistakes and, boy, did I make some doozies! One was particularly memorable. I had invited ten-year-old Marie-Claire Bourque to join me for the first 30 minutes of the noon-hour program. Marie-Claire was a figure skating prodigy from St. Anne du Ruisseau, a community about twenty minutes outside of Yarmouth. She had just won a provincial title, and was visiting me in the studio to tell me all about it. I still have the interview on tape, and am pleased now to provide you with this word-for-word transcript...

"Hi, Marie-Claire, welcome to 'Rainnie at Noon.'"

"Thanks."

"So, tell me, was it fun to win the provincial figure skating title?"

"Yes."

"Were you really happy?"

"Yes."

"Do you love figure skating?"

"Yes."

"Is it one of your favourite things to do?"

"Yes."

"Do you think you'll go to the Canada Games someday?"

"I don't know."

So, there I was, 28 seconds into the interview, with 29-plus minutes still to come, and pretty much all out of ideas. And it was 100 per cent my fault. Marie-Claire was just answering what she was asked. The problem was, my questions were brutally bad. I came to a realization that day that has stood me in fairly good stead since: never (especially when talking to little kids or a guest who is clearly nervous) ask a question that can be answered with a simple "yes" or "no." Because, more often than not, that's exactly what you'll get. Instead, ask questions that begin with one of three interrogative pronouns: "What," "How," or "Why." These force your guest to go beyond the simple one-word answer and actually give you something with a bit of substance. If I could somehow have a do-over with Marie-Claire, better questions would be...

"What was it like when you won the provincial title?"

"How did you feel when they put that medal around your neck?"

"Why do you love figure skating so much?"

"What's your favourite part about the sport?"

"What are your dreams when you think about figure skating?"

No doubt, these would have elicited far more entertaining responses from my sweet little guest. Marie-Claire, if you're reading this, I'm sorry for messing up. On the bright side, though, you did teach me a valuable lesson.

My time at CJLS went well beyond developmental, however. It also provided me with great answers to the one question you inevitably get asked when you speak to kids at schools...

"What's the funniest thing that's ever happened to you while you've been 'live' on the air?"

Well, in no particular order, here are three gems...

1) If you've ever listened to small town radio, then you're likely familiar with the concept of "swap shop." Some stations call it "Buy, Sell, and Trade," others call it "Radio Classified." The name may change, but the principle stays the same: listeners have the chance to sell or solicit goods or services over the airwaves. In Yarmouth, "swap shop" was crazily popular. In fact, what would happen on occasion is that a single person would present a list of items so long that the entire 3-minute segment would be eaten up before having the chance to move on to the next caller. Thus, we were forced to institute a key rule: if you appeared on "swap shop," you would be allowed a maximum of three items per call. This seemed fair, easy to enforce, and seemingly easy to understand.

The new edict couldn't have been any more than a week old when the memorable moment occurred. I was presiding over swap shop and had only just recited the criteria when I welcomed the first caller to the program...

"Hi there, good morning, you're on swap shop!"

A thickly accented French voice replied, "Ahhhh, allo, allo der..."

"Yes, sir, you're on swap shop, go ahead."

"Okay den, I have FOUR items for sale."

Feeling sympathy for the caller but also knowing I was beholden to enforce the new standards, I replied in as soothing a way as possible, "I'm sorry, sir, but as of last week, we now only allow a maximum of THREE items per call."

There was a significant pause on the other end of the line, probably 3 to 4 seconds, before the caller finally responded...

"Okay, den," he said, the resignation palpable in his voice. "I have THREE TIRES for sale."

A classic!

2) For the duration of my time in Yarmouth, and for countless years both before and after, the mayor was a man by the name of Charles Crosby. I had immense admiration for him. He was your typically outstanding small-town leader – he knew everybody by name and was extremely accessible and eminently approachable. I'm unsure about his level of formal education, but I am certain of this: he had a PhD when it came to civic matters and common sense. I've seldom seen a politician more in tune with his community. It's like his finger was constantly taking the pulse of the town.

The only times I ever saw him struggle were in interview situations, where he would occasionally resort to using words that were perhaps beyond the natural parameters of his vocabulary. He was, at times, a master of malapropisms – so skilled, in fact, he would give Yogi Berra or George W. Bush a serious run for their money. What follows are two of my favourite examples...

This one particular summer (I'm pretty sure it was 1994), the Town of Yarmouth had a smelly situation. Citizens were taking their dogs for walks and, in alarmingly large numbers, were not picking up after them. For a tourist destination and gateway to Canada, this presented problems on both the visual and olfactory levels. Things got so bad that Yarmouth Town Council was forced to enact a by-law. I invited the Mayor to join me on my radio show to talk about this controversial issue, and he accepted without hesitation.

On the day of the interview, he stormed into the studio, his stride purposeful and his face a mix of frustration and consternation. I could tell his level of exasperation was high. I turned our microphones on and gingerly welcomed him to the program...

"Mr. Mayor, good of you to be here, and you have a topic you're very anxious to discuss today..."

"You're darn right I do, Bruce," he replied. "I never thought it would come to this, but it has. To preserve the beauty and aroma of our town, the council has been forced to bring in some new legislation."

"And just what does the legislation entail, Your Worship?"

"Bruce, it's simple. Here's the rule: if you take your dog for a walk, and the dog drops its FETUSES on the sidewalk, you bend down and you pick up the FETUSES. Simple as that!"

I was just a young man at the time, but was still seasoned enough to know that something had gone horribly awry. I quickly replayed what he had just said in my head, and was startled when I came to the offending word. As tenderly as possible, I tried to salvage the situation...

"Of course, Mr. Crosby, that's understandable. You want the citizens of Yarmouth to be more diligent in picking up their dogs' FECES."

Not missing a beat, he continued, "That's right, pick up the FETUSES."

And then, to wrap it all up in a pretty little bow, he closed with this whopper...

"Because we on Town Council aren't gonna be held reliable for this anymore!!"

3) During the Yarmouth Mayoral Race of 1994, two brave but ultimately foolhardy souls had the temerity to challenge Mr. Crosby for the town's top job. Late in the campaign, I had the three contenders appear on the "Rainnie at Noon" show for a live debate. The format was fairly loose, and I decided after a few opening questions to open up the phone lines to allow the listeners to dictate the topics that would be discussed. The very first call began as follows...

"I have a question for the incumbent, Mayor Crosby," said a female voice.

"Yes, dear, you go right ahead," he replied.

"Before I can cast my vote for you, I need to know where you stand on an issue that is very important to me."

Prepared at this moment to win this woman over, the mayor said with confidence, "Well, you ask me the question, and I'll answer you as honestly as I can."

"Fine, then," she said. "Mr. Crosby, would you tell me in no uncertain terms: what are your views on euthanasia?"

The Mayor shifted somewhat uncomfortably in his seat, and brought both hands to the table as if to brace himself. He took a look at me, and then a quick look at each of the other two candidates. Taking a deep breath, he finally uttered words that remain etched in my memory some seventeen years later...

"Ma'am, I appreciate the question, I really do. And I truly appreciate your concern as well. But I'm here to tell you today that I am more concerned about YOUTH IN YARMOUTH COUNTY! I JUST DON'T HAVE TIME TO WORRY ABOUT ASIA!"

Gold!

----

*I think today my parents and I would all agree: things have worked out pretty well. But they might not have if my Mom and Dad were anything short of sensational right from the start.

BEST BROADCASTERS
I HAVE SEEN

These are all people I have stood or sat beside when the red light was on. They have all blown me away with their skills as communicators. My choice for #1 is at the top of this list. The rest follow in no particular order.

Ron MacLean

If you asked me today, "Who's the greatest broadcaster you've ever seen?" my answer very quickly would be "Ron MacLean." And I'm fairly certain that if you asked me the same question in thirty or forty years, the answer would be identical. Simply put, Ron MacLean is the seminal broadcaster of my lifetime. And the biggest single reason is this: Ron is EXACTLY the same off-air as he is when the microphone is on. He is the least pretentious and most comfortable person I've ever seen in front of a camera. On top of that, he's a world-class storyteller with a memory that borders on superhuman. His ability to pull a fact from his brain and inject it seamlessly into a story is awe-inspiring.

For a host, Hockey Night in Canada is one of the most frenetic shows in Canadian television. Think of all the varying elements: pre-game show, interviews, highlights from other games, Coach's Corner, Satellite HotStove, post-game show – the list goes on. And week after week, year after year, Ron ties it all together in a manner reminiscent of Marvin Hamlisch conducting the Pittsburgh Philharmonic – with total confidence, total control, and always just the right tone.

Brian Williams

You hear Brian's voice on your TV, and you know something big is about to happen. His delivery is the perfect blend of smoothness and gravitas. Plus, he holds a special place in my heart because of his generosity...

In 2003, I was asked to host the Canada Games for CBC. The games were shared between two cities in New Brunswick, Bathurst and Campbellton. One of my duties was to anchor coverage of the Opening Ceremony. Given that Brian had fronted so many similar such ceremonies at numerous Olympics, I thought it would be invaluable to pick his brain. So we arranged a phone call that I thought might last for 10 to 15 minutes or so. Two hours later, we were still talking! We covered everything, from big thematic broadcast principles ("Less is More," "Silence can be golden") to simple minutiae ("It's just one ceremony, so don't refer to it in plural as the 'Opening Ceremonies'"). Brian was so patient and thorough, and seemed genuinely invested in my upcoming performance. To top it off, a few days before I was to leave for New Brunswick, I received a card in the mail. It was handwritten from Brian, wishing me the best of luck, and recapping all that we had spoken about on the phone. Talk about class...

Matt Rainnie

Before you accuse me of blatant nepotism, let me ask you a question. How many broadcasters do you know who are not just good, but indeed sensational, on BOTH radio and television? The list is pretty short, and it definitely includes my brother. He's funny when it's appropriate, serious when it's called for, easy to listen to, and comfortable to watch. And as a movie reviewer, I can't think of anyone better. Matt could have worked in any market in North America, but chose to stay in the Maritimes for family reasons. We should all be thankful he did...

Terry Leibel

Terry was my partner on Spruce Meadows Show Jumping coverage from 2001 to 2006. In her role as analyst, she was downright clairvoyant, almost to the point of being a bit scary. I can't count how many times a horse and rider would seemingly be cruising along when Terry would yell, "I see trouble!" Sure enough, seconds later, a rail would come down, a perfect ride would come unglued, and nobody saw it all coming but Terry. She was a former Olympic Equestrienne for Canada, and had such an intimate knowledge of the sport. Her ability to communicate that knowledge in a way that was both informative and easy to understand made her one of a kind.

Steve Murphy

The host of the CTV Evening News for the Maritimes is a master. In addition to being one of the best interviewers I've ever seen, Steve has a delivery that is smooth and flawless. You NEVER see him fumble or stumble. That's because he's so well-prepared and so quick on his feet. Steve is also a political junkie, and one of the best election-night hosts in Canada. In fact, I can think of only one who might be better...

Peter Mansbridge

When it comes to hosting elections or special events (Royal Visits, Remembrance Day Celebrations), there is Peter and then there is everybody else. I have worked closely with him on federal elections and Tall Ships visits, and have always been captivated by his commanding voice and presence. He is truly unflappable. He is also extremely giving. In short, he's my favourite type of quarterback: always in full control, but most happy when the rest of his team shines with him.

Boomer Gallant

When Boomer was in grade 4 at St. Jean Elementary School in Charlottetown, Mrs. Hynes asked her students to write an essay. The topic: "What do you want to be when you grow up?" Boomer's answers that day came instantly and, as it turns out, with some clairvoyance. His opening line was, "I want to be a harness racing track announcer and a TV weatherman." Forty-four years later, he's lived both dreams and he's set unmatchable standards of excellence.

If you've never heard Boomer call a horse race, go sometime to YouTube and search "Gold Cup and Saucer." Select any from the 1980s or early 1990s, and give it a listen. When you're finished, I'm sure you'll agree – nobody in North America has ever called a harness race better. And as for TV weather forecasting, here's what I can tell you...

I've worked with Boomer for eight years, and have partnered with him on close to 1,500 Compass programs. In that time, I have never seen him stumble or be at a loss for words. This is remarkable, given that I've also never seen him use a note or a piece of prepared script. I never take for granted that every night I get to work with an outstanding talent and truly memorable TV character.

Scott Russell

Scott and I have worked countless events together (Olympics, Pan American Games, Championship Curling, Spruce Meadows Show Jumping), and beyond being a generous colleague, I would say that he is my best friend at CBC Sports. There are two things that make him stand out. Number one is his passion, especially for amateur sport. Scott is such a fan, and is not afraid to let that emotion leak into his presentation. Number two is his ability with the pen. In my opinion, there is no finer writer working in sport television today. Listen sometime to the opening of a broadcast Scott is hosting. Every word is Scott's, and they flow like poetry. Did I mention, too, that Scott's first job in broadcasting was as a reporter on Compass, the CBC supper-hour show for PEI? With a foundation like that, no wonder he turned out great!

Joan McCusker and Mike Harris

When the legendary CBC broadcaster Don Wittman became seriously ill in the winter of 2007, I was chosen to fill in as lead announcer on coverage of Championship Curling. All involved hoped it would be a temporary assignment. Sadly, however, it became permanent when Don passed away in January of 2008. The transition would have been impossible were it not for the welcoming arms of Joan and Mike, who for my money form the best curling commentary team in the business.

Joan was a member of the great Sandra Schmirler team from Saskatchewan (Olympic Gold Medalists in 1998), and is so in tune with team chemistry. As she watches a game, she can instantly tell when a foursome is really gelling or, by contrast, starting to come apart at the seams.

Mike is also an Olympic Medalist, having skipped the men's team that won silver in 1998. His ability to predict what might happen and then analyze what actually does is unparalleled in Canadian broadcasting.

Mike Duffy

The current senator from PEI is the foremost television political analyst of the last four decades. In that time, he's covered every major political event in Canada and seemingly hasn't forgotten a single detail. He's also keenly aware that he's in the entertainment business, and is not above saying something deliberately controversial to incite good debate.

I've had the pleasure of working with "Duff" a couple of times, and each has been memorable. My confidence level as host is always very high when he's beside me. I know I can go pretty much anywhere topic-wise and he'll be there to not only follow, but enhance.

Russ Anber

Russ is the current boxing analyst for TSN. Before that, he did similar work for CBC. In 2004, he and I were paired for the Olympics in Athens. Outside of Boomer, I don't think I've ever had more immediate chemistry with a broadcast partner. We just hit it off perfectly and became ideal foils for one another. Russ has no formal broadcast training, but he doesn't need it. In fact, it might actually ruin him! He's a total natural, a showman, what I often call "good TV." He's brash, opinionated, eloquent, and knows his sport inside-out. It was both a challenge and privilege working with him and I hope I get the chance again in the not-too-distant future.

Favourite Trivia Question #1

Six brother tandems in NHL history fit the following description: when you look at the combined careers of the two brothers, you find, at some point, time spent with the Montreal Canadiens and a 50-goal season. Name the brother combinations.

BOOMER – "ALTOCUMES"

Boomer invests enormous pride in his weather forecasts and takes it quite personally if even the tiniest detail is slightly off. (Nothing, by the way, gives me more pleasure than pointing out these inaccuracies to Boomer the day after one of his error-laden presentations – it is so much fun watching him explain how things went off the rails.)

As a matter of fact, one of his favourite expressions in life is, "As predicted." Here's how that would work in a conversation. You see Boomer walking down the street and innocently say something like, "Windy day today, Boomer..." He would swagger for a brief moment and then reply, ever so cheekily, "As predicted!"

With that as a backdrop, the following story...

This one August night, we were broadcasting live from the Charlottetown waterfront. Our show was to end that night at 6:30, and, at around 6:28, the most foreboding clouds you've ever seen rolled in almost instantly. The sky darkened to such a degree that our cameraman actually had to turn on some artificial light.

Anyway, I figured now was the time to call Boomer over to explain this rapidly developing weather phenomenon. He didn't hesitate a second in disseminating his meteorological expertise...

"Bruce, these are what we in the weather business like to call alto cumulus clouds, or altocumes for short. Their dominant characteristic is that they appear extremely threatening. But I'm here to assure you that they contain no, I repeat NO, precipitation."

I'm not saying that his forecast was off, but...

Within a half-hour, Canadian Tire had sold out of sump pumps.

People named "Noah" on PEI were beginning to collect animals. It was the biggest monsoon anyone could ever remember, and where was Boomer?

Hiding at home in his basement, his phone off the hook for the night.

The legacy of the "altocumes" event lives on. To this day, anytime Boomer now mentions these cloud formations during a weather forecast, you can detect the very faint smile in his voice. He knows we're both thinking the exact same thing: NO PRECIPITATION WHATSOEVER!

ISLANDERS I THOROUGHLY ENJOY SPEAKING WITH
(IN NO PARTICULAR ORDER)

Interviews make up a big part of our Compass program. We generally do two, sometimes three, per night. Some are conversational in nature, some are more accountability driven. In terms of style, every interviewer has his/her own. Some are aggressive, even abrasive (Jim Nunn, Bill O'Reilly). Some are tough, but always fair (Peter Mansbridge, Bob Costas, Steve Murphy). And some are softer and less confrontational (Larry King, Jay Leno). I'm not sure where I fit, but I hope it's somewhere near the "tough but fair" category.

I will share with you my two goals for every interview I do on CBC. Number one, I work extremely hard to determine, and then ask, the three or four key questions that you at home would like to see answered. And, number two, and most important, no matter the tone of the interview, I try to treat the person across from me with respect. I hope that if you've been a guest on Compass, you've left with your dignity intact.

Here are some of my favourites.

Ron MacKinley

There is nothing quite like a "live" interview with Mr. MacKinley. Four times he's graced me with his presence on the Compass set, and each has been, shall we say, memorable. He's one-of-a-kind, a master of malapropisms, and always at least a step ahead of you. When (if) he retires from politics, I hope he'll join me for a weekly Friday segment on CBC. We could call it "Rappin' with Ronnie," and just discuss whatever's on his mind. Tell me you wouldn't tune in for that!

Lorie Kane

When I talk to Lorie, I always feel constrained by TV time limits. I could listen to her for hours. What is most impressive to me is that she's always had a clear sense of where she wants to go, but she's never forgotten where she's been. She loves her home province, and makes no attempt to hide it.

Alex Campbell

The former premier is the personification of dignity and class. Spend just a few minutes with him and you readily understand why he was the longest-serving premier in PEI history.

Robert Ghiz

He is the first premier I've ever interviewed who is of my generation. Further to that, we are both relatively new fathers, both enjoy sports, and both relish a good laugh. He has a good sense of humour and is always very well prepared. My interviews with him have ranged from conversational to challenging, and I've enjoyed them all.

Brad Richards

Here he is, one of the NHL's brightest and best-paid stars, and yet he's content to shine silently. It's like pulling teeth trying to get him to talk about himself, but I'm still glad he gives me the chance whenever I call.

Charlottetown Mayor Clifford Lee

He's very accessible, and has an undeniable affection for his city. He's also that rare politician who always gives you the straightest answer he can.

Al MacAdam

The former NHL star is very thoughtful, and never resorts to clichés. He tells it exactly as he sees it, and does not suffer foolish questions gladly. This is really all you could ever ask for in a guest.

Jen Nicholson

Jen is a mother of three from Cornwall who in the past half-decade has become one of the premier marathon runners in Canada. She was the top Canadian female at the 2011 Boston Marathon, posting a personal best time of 2 hours, 47 minutes. I've only had the opportunity to interview her once, and was so impressed with her eloquence, passion, and humility.

Dr. Heather Morrison

Very measured and articulate, she was the very definition of grace under pressure during the H1N1 scare of 2009. In every interview, she brought exactly the right tone, leaving Islanders with the comforting sense that we'd get through this, and that everything would be okay.

Adam McQuaid

This young man so impressed me in the months after his Stanley Cup win with the Boston Bruins, he could have come home, closed his door, and hidden. Many in his position would have after a long and exhausting hockey season. But instead, he made himself accessible – to kids, to events, to charities, and to communities across the Island. Gracious, thoughtful, and so proud to be from PEI, this gentle giant is a model ambassador for Canada's smallest province.

Pat Binns

The first time I ever interviewed the former premier, I thought I really ticked him off with my very first question. I don't remember the question exactly, but I do remember that he just stared at me for what seemed like seconds, saying nothing. I soon realized that this wasn't a sign of disdain, but instead his pattern. He actually was taking a moment to formulate his thoughts before offering an answer. I never mistook his soft-spoken nature for a lack of toughness.

Jared Connaughton

The Olympic Sprinter from New Haven, PEI, always makes time for Compass, no matter where he is in the world. He's very expressive, has a great rhythm to his speech, and clearly loves what he does.

BAPTISM BY FIRE – FIRST TIME ON HOCKEY NIGHT

If you're a broadcaster in Canada, and you have even the faintest interest in sports, then there is one program, and really ONLY one, that you truly yearn to work for. And when that day finally comes, after you've wondered for years if it ever will – well, you're not likely to forget a single detail. For me, the date was February 9, 2002; the place was Air Canada Centre in Toronto; the teams were the Montreal Canadiens and Toronto Maple Leafs; and the stage was, of course, Hockey Night in Canada. But before I share with you the particulars of that day, a bit of back story...

In January of 2002, Windsor, Nova Scotia, was the host town for CBC's annual special daylong broadcast, Hockey Day in Canada. I was given a fairly significant on-air role that day, and reported from various events in and around the Windsor area. I also had the opportunity to spend a good chunk of the afternoon with Ron MacLean and Don Cherry. I had met Ron before and knew him a little, but this was my first extended time in the presence of "Grapes." And oh how we jelled!

"You know, Mr. Cherry," I said, "I have to agree with you – Bobby Orr was the best to ever play the game."

"Wasn't he a beauty? The greatest, boy, the greatest...Parry Sound...Bobby Orr...the best, I tell ya, THE BEST!!"

"But you know," I continued, "my favourite player growing up was Guy Lafleur. Did you like him?"

"Like him?" he replied, "Did I like him? That S.O.B. cost me two Stanley Cups. But I loved Guy – never complained, never whined.

Thurso, Quebec – hair flyin' in the wind...great fella, GREAT FELLA!"

And on and on it went for the better part of an hour. What tremendous and undeniable rapport we had! By the end of our conversation, I was convinced we had laid the groundwork for a potentially meaningful and enduring "bromance."

At the very end of the day, when the marathon broadcast had concluded, everyone gathered in a private room for a small celebration. I was enjoying some broccoli and dip when Hockey Night producer Joel Darling made his way through a throng of people and asked to speak with me for a moment.

"You did a really nice job today," he said.

"Oh, thanks, Joel," I replied. "It was a lot of fun to be involved with this."

"Listen," he said. "I was wondering – what are you doing on Saturday, February 9?"

"Well, it's strange that you ask, but I have tickets that day to see Billy Joel and Elton John together at the Bell Centre in Montreal. Should be an awesome concert..."

"Oh, well, that's too bad. Because I was going to ask you if you wanted to work on Hockey Night in Canada that day. Montreal is playing in Toronto."

(Silence... More silence... Extended silence... Then...)

"Well, I'd love to, but these tickets were really hard to get, and I've really been looking forward to this show. Billy Joel is one of my all-time favourite musicians."

(More silence, as Joel just stares at me...)

"I suppose I could see this concert time some other time, though."

(Joel starts to slowly nod his head...)

"I suppose I could actually give the tickets to my Mom and Dad as a sort of unplanned gift."

(Joel continues to nod...)

"I guess I really shouldn't pass up this opportunity. After all, who knows when it will come again?"

(Joel still nodding...)

"More to the point, who knows if it will come again?"

(Joel nodding vigorously now...)

"You know, after giving it some thought, I think I'd like to work on Hockey Night in Canada on February 9."

Joel stops nodding. "That's a wise decision, Bruce. Glad we were able to make it happen." (For the record, elapsed time for this complete flip-flop was at most 15 seconds. That has to be some sort of record...)

And so, it was an afternoon matchup at Air Canada Centre, and it was my first time ever in that building to see a hockey game. I'll never forget the feeling walking inside to get my media credentials and then walking downstairs to the Hockey Night in Canada studio. I remember unpacking my briefcase, organizing some notes on the desk, and thinking, "How could this get any more surreal?" That question was answered mere moments later when a voice from the doorway said, "Hey, I hear you're making your debut on Hockey Night in Canada today. I just wanted to wish you good luck."

Looking up, I was stunned to suddenly be making eye contact with Toronto Maple Leaf President and Hockey Hall of Fame goalie, Ken Dryden.

"Thanks, Mr. Dryden," I stammered, extending my hand. "It sure is nice to meet you. And thanks so much for dropping by."

"Not a problem," he said. "What exactly are you doing on the show today?"

A good question, and I'll tell you now what I told him then. My job that day was to work as rinkside reporter. Ron MacLean was actually in Salt Lake City preparing for the 2002 Winter Olympics, but he was still able to host the broadcast "via satellite." My job was to find out who was playing, who was injured, and to interview players during the intermissions and after the game.

We came on the air at 3:00 p.m. sharp, and, about 40 seconds later, Ron threw it to me for my first ever "hit" on Hockey Night in Canada. Standing in the hallway outside the Leafs' dressing room, my hand was shaky, my voice even shakier, but I gave the injury updates and made it to the end mostly without incident. I concluded with a very clever and creative, "Back to you, Ron."

At this point, I thought I had time to reflect and relax and bask in the glow. After all, according to the script, I wouldn't be appearing again for some 45 minutes, until the first intermission. The serenity of the moment was quickly shattered, however, when my floor director, Mike Christiansen, grabbed me by the arm and sternly said, "C'mon, we've got to get back to the studio."

"Why the rush?" I asked.

"Just be quiet and come with me," was his terse reply.

When we reached the studio, Mike pointed to the chair normally occupied by Ron MacLean and said, "Hurry up and sit down."

Now you'll never guess who was in a chair just a few feet away, getting his makeup done and fixing his vast collar. That's right, none other than the man with whom I so successfully bonded some scant thirty days ago in Nova Scotia, the star of "Coach's Corner," the legend himself, Mr. Don Cherry.

"Hi, Mr. Cherry," I offered. "Remember me? We spent the day together in Windsor about a month ago."

"Hey, how ya' doin'? Yeah, yeah, good to see you again,"

"Bruce, I gotta interrupt,' said Mike. "Listen, something got screwed up, and we're coming back from commercial during the anthem. We can't go to ice level for just part of 'O Canada' – that would be disrespectful. So, you're going to have to fill time for about 45 seconds."

"OK, "I said. " What would you like me to talk about?"

Mike's response was not exactly what I was looking for? "5, 4, 3, 2, 1... Cue!"

Stunned, I looked straight ahead to find the red light on top of the big camera staring back at me. In my ear, I heard the producer say,

"Go, Bruce, you're on!"

With sweat beads instantaneously beginning to crystallize on my brow, I dove headfirst into some seriously uncharted, murky, and choppy water...

"Welcome back to Air Canada Centre in Toronto, and a special matinee matchup between the Montreal Canadiens and Toronto Maple Leafs."

An acceptable start, but I still had 40 seconds to go. It's a bit foggy from this point forward, but I do remember next highlighting the two goalies – José Theodore of Montreal, who was midway through what would turn out to be an MVP season, and Curtis Joseph of Toronto, who just a week later would be the starting goalie for Team Canada in its first game at the 2002 Olympics. Trouble was, I was speaking so bloody fast that I was hardly chewing up any time at all...

"Thirty seconds to puck drop, Bruce," came that bothersome voice in my ear.

At this point, two things happened. Firstly, big drops of sweat began to fall at about 3-second intervals from my right eyebrow onto the desk in front of me. Seriously, you can clearly see this on the videotape, and it's hilarious. Secondly, I dug deep into my well of hockey knowledge (in retrospect, way too deep) to fill the remaining time...

"You know, Mats Sundin of the Leafs is having by far his best season in Toronto. As a matter of fact, right now, he's third in league scoring. Now, if he can somehow reach the top position and stay there, he could become the first Leaf since Gordie Drillon in 1938 to win the NHL scoring title. And wouldn't that be something..."

I realize now that going back to the late 1930s and bringing up some guy that three-quarters of the audience had never heard of is not the ideal way to set up an important matchup in the early 2000s. But hey, when you're drowning, you'll grasp for anything. Plus, it allowed me to reach the instant where I finally heard the eleven words that were pure magic to my sweat-soaked ears...

"Ten seconds left, you can throw it to the guys upstairs."

Deliverance!

"And so the stage is set for the latest chapter in hockey's most enduring rivalry. To call the action, let's head upstairs to join Bob Cole and Harry Neale."

And with that, the red light went off and the weight of the world lifted from my shoulders. Taking a deep sigh, I buried my face in my hands, shook my head back and forth for at least a minute, and muttered, "Good Lord, what just happened?"

Watching my anguish unfold from his chair just an arm's length away was, you guessed it, Mr. Don Cherry. Reaching out with his right hand, he grabbed me by the shoulder, turned me ever so slightly toward him, looked me square in the eye, and channeling the great Judy Garland, uttered words that remain frozen in my memory: "Ha! I guess you're not in Windsor anymore, Brian!"

And, with that, a swift and sudden end to the budding "bromance!"

Don actually called me "Brian" for the entire rest of the day. And instead of correcting him, I just figured it would be easier to answer to it. Plus, it would make the story better. As a matter of fact, when I got home, I couldn't wait to e-mail Ron MacLean to share with him this case of mistaken identity.

His response came back almost immediately, had me laughing for a good ten minutes, and somehow made me feel 100 per cent better about my Hockey Night initiation...

"Remember, Bruce, Don is living proof that you can be a huge success in this country without speaking either of the two official languages."

MacLean is the best!

Favourite Trivia Question #2

Eight players in NHL history scored 500 goals while playing their entire careers for ONLY one team. Name them.

THE FLOWER

I get asked often, "What's the best part of your job?"

The answer to that is simple. It's the people you get to meet and talk to on a daily basis. And to take it one step further – in many cases, these are people you would likely never meet if you were working in most any other occupation.

For example, in the last twenty-six years, I've had the good fortune to interview Canadian prime ministers, a US president, provincial premiers, Olympic gold medalists, figure skating stars, hockey legends, curling stalwarts, business titans, and entertainment icons.

When I recite this list for kids at schools, invariably a hand will extend into the air, and this question will follow: "Did any of them make you nervous?"

I can honestly say that none did. I was excited prior to each of these interviews, but not, by definition, really nervous.

The only time I was truly knee-shaking, palm-sweating, mouth-dry, basket-case nervous was when I had the chance to interview my boyhood idol. You might have heard of him. Wore #10. Played for the Montreal Canadiens. Led the team to four straight Stanley Cups in the late 70s. Was a fixture every Saturday night on Hockey Night in Canada. Had a great nickname: "The Flower." And, to this day, he was the most exciting hockey player I've ever seen. Not the best, mind you – I begrudgingly admit that Orr, Gretzky, Lemieux, and Messier were all probably better. But none could match the flair, panache, and style of Guy Lafleur. He was breathtaking – an artist who inspired broadcasters and fellow players.

Guy Lafleur's prime lasted for six years, from 1974–75 to 1979–80. I was seven when he had his first 50-goal season, and thirteen when he had his last. These are impressionable times for a young boy, the ages where heroes take form and shape. Guy Lafleur was mine.

I apologize to those of you of religious persuasion, but I must be honest. As a little boy, the Holy Trinity for me was really a Holy Quartet, with Lafleur as the fourth and the order constantly in flux. I worshipped him. I prayed nightly he would score a goal (these prayers were usually answered). And I dreamed someday of meeting him, and always wondered what I would say.

Fast forward to 1996. Guy Lafleur had been retired for a few years, and I was working as a host at CBC in Halifax. Word leaked that Lafleur would be special guest player at an upcoming Oldtimers game at the Halifax Metro Centre. I figured, now's my chance. I called the people in charge of the event to book an interview with the great Guy Lafleur. They said it would not be a problem, and gave me his hotel and a time.

On the day of the interview, I was bouncing. Couldn't eat breakfast or lunch, couldn't sit still, couldn't wait! At the agreed-upon time, my cameraman, Eric Woolliscroft, and I arrived at the hotel ready for the chance of a lifetime. We approached the woman at the desk and told her we were there to interview Guy Lafleur. She looked at us, removed her glasses, and said, "I'm sorry, but the Oldtimers' plane has been delayed because of weather. The players will have to go straight to the rink when they arrive in Halifax. So, I'm afraid this interview won't happen."

I was crestfallen, my mouth agape. Eric had to lead me, arm in arm, staggering, back to our vehicle. I couldn't talk, could barely breathe. Eric finally said, "Let's go back to your house and have something to drink."

We arrived, cracked open a couple of cans of Diet Pepsi, and sat there in the silence in the dark. Finally, Eric said, "I can't take this anymore. Call the hotel and see if anything's changed. You never know."

In the most mature way possible, I looked at Eric and said, "I'm not calling the damn hotel."

He said, "C'mon, what do we have to lose?"

Again, in a very mature way, I said, "Fine then."

Deliberately, I dialed the number, and the same woman answered. I reintroduced myself, and asked if anything had changed. Her next sentence came at me in a way that saw my heart rate increase five beats per each word! She said, "Oh, yes, Guy Lafleur just checked in. He arrived on a different flight. I'll put you through to his room."

I looked at Eric, my eyes the size of large dinner plates. He said, "What?" I cleverly replied, "Shut up!" (Surprisingly, Eric and I are still the best of friends. This says a lot about him.)

Seconds seemed like hours as I waited to hear whether anyone would pick up on the other end of the line. Sweat by that point had assumed permanent residency on both my brows and upper lip. Finally, a click, and a voice...

"Allo."

It was voice I instantly recognized from myriad Hockey Night in Canada 1st intermission interviews in the late 1970s. Very deep, very French.

My initial response was sit to sit there, hold the phone, and say nothing. Again, I heard...

"Allo."

Remember, please, that by this point I had spent most of living years hoping desperately to someday talk to Guy Lafleur. I always dreamed of how the conversation might go. And now, presented with the opportunity of a lifetime, here was the best a normally quite self-assured professional broadcaster could come up with...

"Mr. Lafleur??"

"Yes."

"Hi…my name is…GUY Rainnie." (Eric falls off chair onto floor in convulsive laughter…)

"Your name is Guy, too??"

Scrambling now, I say, "No, I'm just really excited to talk to you, and I screwed up. My name is really Bruce." (Eric now clutching his stomach…)

Silence, and then a little laugh from the Flower, "Hee, hee, hee."

Now my competitive juices kick in, and I realize I must act quickly to save this rapidly disintegrating situation. I figure, I'll impress him with my knowledge…

"I remember in six straight years you scored 53, 56, 56, 60, 52, and 50 goals."

(Silence)

"Six straight years with at least 50 goals!"

(Silence)

"That's pretty awesome." (Eric now making beeline to washroom…)

Lafleur pauses, and then thankfully breaks the silence with, "I didn't even know that – maybe you should get a life or something! Hee, hee, hee…"

To make a long story short (perhaps it's too late for that now), we ended up in Guy Lafleur's hotel room for an interview that is still a career highlight for me. He could not have been more patient, classy, or kind. And when the interview was over, he sat with us for what must have been another 45 minutes, just telling old stories and answering any extra questions we had. It was magical!

It's an amazing and rare feeling when your idol turns out to be an even better person than he was a player.

Thank you, Guy Lafleur, for memories, both on- and off-ice, that will last a lifetime.

By the way, I have seen Guy Lafleur many times since that initial encounter, and, unlike me, he's never forgotten my name. Must have made some sort of memorable impression.

MOST IMPRESSIVE ATHLETES
I HAVE SEEN IN PERSON

Heather Moyse

Here's a telltale musing on the overwhelming athleticism of Heather Moyse. Prior to the 2010 Olympics in Vancouver, Heather was home in Summerside and working out in a local gym. She was following a program prescribed for her by her trainer, and, boy, was she having a tough time with her single-leg squats! She was able to do her sets of 6, but it was more tortuous and exhausting than she ever imagined. So grueling, in fact, that Heather actually grew concerned about what she perceived as a sudden lack of power and conditioning.

That night, she called her coach, and told him of her crisis. "Matt," she said, "I was able to so the reps, but I'm really worried. I actually found this exercise hard to do with 70 kilograms on the bar."

Silence from the other end of the line, until Matt replied, laughing, "Heather, I gave you these exercises in 'pounds' and not 'kilograms!'"

(There are 2.2 pounds in a kilogram, so Heather was actually doing these single leg squats with 154 pounds!)

Matt concluded by saying, "Take tomorrow off, Heather. We're not going to really concern ourselves about your strength!"

Sidney Crosby

Two things strike you about Sidney Crosby when you see him play hockey up close. Number one is the lower body strength. His upper thighs and haunches are just massive, and are the engines that drive the most dynamic skating stride in the game. Number two is the focus. You can see it in his eyes. He never takes a shift off, and always leaves the ice fully spent.

Daniel Igali

At the 2000 Olympics in Sydney, Australia, Daniel Igali won gold for Canada in the 69 kg men's freestyle wrestling division. In fact, one of the indelible moments in Canadian Olympic history is of Igali so proudly circling a maple-leaf flag on the wrestling mat in Sydney before kneeling down to kiss it, and then dissolving into tears when the medal was placed around his neck.

I had the honour of calling that gold-medal performance for CBC Sports, and of getting to know Daniel Igali fairly well. Here was a guy who stood maybe 5'7" tall, and weighed in the neighbourhood of 155 pounds. But what a powerhouse! In training, I saw him bench press over 300 pounds, sprint 100 metres in just under 11 seconds, and vertically leap over 40 inches into the air. Awe-inspiring...

Reggie Jackson

Back in 1980, my mother actually won a trip for two to Boston to see a September series between the Red Sox and Yankees. In true selfless-mom fashion, she let my Dad and me go. What a thrill it was for a thirteen-year- old – my first ever big-time sporting event, and it's the Yanks and Sox at Fenway Park. Tough to beat that.

I remember every detail of that trip to this day, and what still resonates strongest is the show that Reggie Jackson put on in batting practice. He sent pitch after pitch (at least 12-13 in a row) soaring deep into the bleachers in right-centre field. And what made it even more memorable is that between swings he would stop and playfully taunt the Red Sox fans who were giving him a hard time. It was a truly captivating powerhitting/comedy exhibition, and, in retrospect, it's refreshing to know it wasn't steroid-aided.

Eric Lindros

To see Eric Lindros in person was awe-inspiring. If possible, he was even bigger than he looked on TV, with a body that seemed sculpted from granite. Seriously, he was built along the lines of an Arnold Schwarzenegger. He could also skate like the wind and shoot a puck with tremendous force and accuracy. We are left to wonder just how great he could have been had injuries and concussions not shortened his time at the top.

I know that many hockey fans found Lindros a hard guy to warm up to. He came into the league under a cloud of controversy and never really emerged from it. He was, however, an extremely generous, kind, and quiet guy. I saw him once at a celebrity golf event in Nova Scotia, and what he did blew me away. There was an afternoon set aside for the celebrities to sign autographs for some local kids. It was extremely hot and humid and there was very little shade. The session was supposed to last two hours, but most of the celebrities quietly and slyly slipped away after forty-five minutes. Not Lindros. At the height of his fame there he stood, until every young person had an autograph, a photo, a handshake, whatever. Pretty impressive...

Ben Cahoon

When the CFL was on CBC, I worked as a field reporter for what must have been twenty-five games over a three-year period. Because of proximity to PEI, the team I saw the most was the Montreal Alouettes. And the player who always blew me away was Montreal's superlative slotback, #86, Ben Cahoon. What was most impressive about Cahoon was just how unimpressive he was physically. He wasn't very big, wasn't very fast, and by his own admission couldn't jump a lick. What made him so great was an unprecedented combination of determination and hand-eye coordination. He could catch anything and would make every effort to do so. The result? He retired as the all-time leading pass catcher in CFL history.

Roger Federer

Forget for a moment the tennis skill, which is outrageous. What stands out for me having watched Federer play in the midsummer sweltering heat of Montreal or Toronto is that he never breaks a sweat. His movement is so precise and economical that he seldom even appears out of breath.

My lasting impression of Federer, though, comes from the 2007 Rogers Cup played in Montreal. His opponent in the final was the talented Serbian player Novak Djokovic. Djokovic won the first set in a tiebreak, 7-6. Federer won the second 6-2. In a match that stretched close to three hours on a scorching afternoon, Djokovic won the third set in another tiebreak. After the trophy presentations had concluded, we signed off and said goodbye for another year. As I was packing up my pens and notes, my broadcast partner, Peter Burwash, tapped me on the shoulder and said, "Look at what's going on at centre court." As I gazed downward, there was Federer (who had lost, remember), some forty-five minutes after the final point had been played, posing for pictures with all of the ball boys and ball girls. Not one young kid was denied. Burwash looked at me and said, "Right there – that's why men's tennis is in such good shape. What a guy to be leading the way..."

Hayley Wickenheiser

Prior to the 2006 Winter Olympics in Torino, Italy, there were quiet whispers that Hayley Wickenheiser's game had slipped ever so slightly, and that Krissy Wendell of the USA had usurped as the premier player in women's hockey. I remember asking Hayley about this prior to the start of the Games, and her answer was telling. She said, "I wouldn't write me off just yet..."

More prophetic words were never spoken. In five games at those Olympics she scored 5 goals and 12 assists for 17 points, led Canada to a gold medal, and was the unanimous choice for tournament MVP.

I remember heading downstairs to offer congratulations to the Canadian women after the medals had been handed out. One of the first players I saw was Wickenheiser, who curiously extended her left hand to shake mine. I wondered why until I looked at her right hand and saw that it was encased in a makeshift cast. Turns out she had played the entire Olympic tournament with a broken right wrist, and totally dominated.

She is without doubt the greatest female hockey player of all time, and the gap between #1 and #2 is gargantuan.

Catriona Le May Doan

Catriona Le May Doan retired from her remarkable competitive speed skating career in the winter of 2003, and began her very promising broadcasting career months later with CBC at the 2003 Pan American Games in Santo Domingo, Dominican Republic. I was also part of that CBC team, and hit it off immediately with Catriona. I found her funny, brilliant, and eager to soak up all she could about broadcasting.

During those games, I helped Catriona produce a feature on inline skating (roller blading is the more common name), which is a sanctioned sport at Pan Am Games. We thought it would be neat to have Catriona actually train for an afternoon with the Canadian team, to see how challenging it would be for a speed skater to adapt to a totally new discipline. At that point in her life, she had never before even put on a pair of rollerskates. Well, in the span of about twenty minutes, she went from tentative, to comfortable, to proficient, to expert. It was awe-inspiring to watch the transformation. At the end of the session, the Canadian coach actually took me aside and told me he thought she could win a medal if she trained for another day or so. That, my friends, is an athlete.

Kevin Martin

I've been part of the CBC broadcast team for curling since late 2007, and can honestly say that you have to watch this sport live to truly appreciate the strategy and otherworldly skill involved. What the very best in the world can do with a 40-pound piece of granite is extraordinary. That being said, one player, in my opinion, stands alone at the top of the heap and continually leaves me searching for words to describe what he's just done. He is Olympic champion Kevin Martin of Edmonton, Alberta, a bona fide curling savant and probably the greatest to ever play the game. He is so clever and strong, and can alternately throw the stone with feathery finesse or overwhelming power. If you ever have the chance to see him play, take it. You won't be disappointed.

SID AND *DUENDE*

Chances are, you've never heard of one of my all-time favourite writers. His name was George Frazier (1911–1974), and the bulk of his career was spent as a columnist for *The Boston Globe*. The sole reason I ever came across him is because of my fascination (my wife would say obsession) with Richard Nixon and Watergate. In my readings on the subject, I learned that the famously paranoid Nixon had an "enemies list," people he considered legitimate threats to his presidency. On this list was Frazier. Out of curiosity, I "Googled" him and found links to a number of his columns (many of which eviscerated Nixon in an almost artistic way). If you enjoy writing that is laden with style, colour, and acerbic wit, I urge you to do the same. You won't be disappointed.

Frazier wrote often of something he called *duende*. When asked to define it, he struggled, but settled on "that certain something that sets persons apart. It might be 'soul,' but it might also be 'star quality.' It is a power that transmits a profound feeling from the heart of the artist to his audience with the minimum of fuss and the maximum of restraint."

Frazier first sensed and wrote of *duende* when he saw Joe DiMaggio grace an outfield. It wasn't merely greatness that he saw, nor majesty, nor aura. It was *duende*, and he had to learn more about it. "To say that *duende* is simply charisma or panache or flair is rather to demean it," Frazier wrote, "for while it is certainly all those things, it is the nth power of them. It is chemistry."

Frazier's definition of *duende* evolved through his prose and, more clearly, through example. "Clark Gable," Frazier wrote in his first lecture on *duende*, "had that certain something but others, like Rock Hudson, do not." In Frazier's view, Ingrid Bergman had *duende*. So did Billie Holliday. Fred Astaire had it, but not Gene Kelly. "It was what Ted Williams had even when striking out, but Stan Musial lacked when hitting a home run," wrote Frazier.

Modern day, I would suggest that Frazier would say David Letterman has *duende*, but Jay Leno doesn't. Clint Eastwood yes, Robert Redford no. George Clooney for certain, Matt Damon less certain. Barbra Steisand affirmative, Celine Dion negative. Tiger Woods of 2008 definitely, Tiger Woods of 2011 definitely not. I'm sure by now you get the point. Which brings me to the subject of this chapter: Sidney Patrick Crosby of Cole Harbour, Nova Scotia.

I've found myself thinking a lot these past few years about what Mr. Frazier would think of young Mr. Crosby. I feel fairly safe in saying he would find Sidney overflowing with *duende*. In fact, he would probably write that he oozes it. And he'd be bang on.

I've had the privilege of working as a rinkside reporter for close to a hundred NHL games over the last decade. Twelve of those games have featured Sidney Crosby and the Pittsburgh Penguins. Let me assure you, when Crosby and the Pens come to town, it brings a totally different ambiance to the arena. For example, at a typical Saturday night game in Toronto (say between the Leafs and the Sabres), teams take to the ice at 6:30 sharp for a pre-game skate. Generally at this time, the stands are about two-thirds empty and gradually fill to capacity by the time the puck is dropped at 7:10. But when Pittsburgh is in Toronto, you look around at 6:30 and realize that 95 per cent of the fans have already arrived. And, man, are they pumped! So many flashbulbs are going off that you'd swear a massive lightning storm was actually taking place inside the arena. Every male fan, no matter the age, looks downright giddy. Every female fan, no matter the age, looks like she spent an extra fifteen minutes getting ready. Little kids press their freckled, gap-toothed faces against the Plexiglas, pens, programs, and photos clutched in their anxious fingers, hoping that Sidney will suddenly abandon the warm-up, leave the ice, and jump into the stands to start signing. It's a wondrous thing to witness up close, and it has to be the very definition of *duende*. And the amazing thing is that this kid has had it since he was, well, a kid.

I go back a long way with Sidney Crosby. I first heard of him in 1995, when I was working as the late-night sports anchor for the CBC in Halifax. I kept getting calls from people in Cole Harbour. Over and over I was told that I had to come do a profile on this eight-year-old hockey phenomenon who was setting scoring records while playing against boys two and three years older. "How good could he really be?" I wondered. Skeptical, but admittedly curious, I finally relented and headed one evening to Cole Harbour Place (the local arena) to watch Sidney play. What I saw stunned me. For one thing, the stands were filled to capacity – this for a minor hockey game. There must have been close to a thousand people there to watch this kid play. And what a show he put on! If memory serves, the Cole Harbour Red Wings beat Shearwater that night by a score of 9 to 4, with Sidney, by far the youngest player on the ice, scoring 4 goals and adding 4 assists. I vividly recall thinking that this was the best young hockey player I had ever seen. It was crystal clear even then (yes, at age eight) that if he grew to a sufficient size and maintained what was an obvious love for the game, professional hockey stardom was inevitable.

As blown way as I was, I chose that night not to put a camera in young Sidney's face. The major contributor to this decision was witnessing what is clearly the dark side of hockey parenting. The performance of a select group was simply appalling. During the game, those on the Shearwater side yelled clever things like "Hot Dog!" or "Nail him!" or "Break his arm!" Shockingly, those on the Cole Harbour side, clearly fueled by jealously, screamed, "Pass the puck, you little puck hog," or "Show-off!" This despite the fact that Sidney spent the entire night trying to set up his less-skilled teammates for goals. Remember, he was eight years old at the time. He just seemed so little and innocent, and I didn't want to put any undue or added pressure on him. I also didn't want to draw any more unwanted attention to him. The timing just didn't seem right for any sort of interview. I knew, however, that this would not always be the case, and vowed to follow his progress from afar.

Fast forward a few years to the 2002 edition of CBC's Hockey Day in Canada. The producers of the show called me a few months prior to the broadcast, looking for a catchy hockey story from Nova Scotia. I suggested a feature on Sidney. He was fourteen by this time and playing with young men two to three years older on the Dartmouth Midget AAA Subways. He was smack dab in the middle of a season that would see him score 95 goals and 98 assists in just 74 games and lead his team to second place nationally at the Air Canada Cup. Still, though, the producers were hesitant, saying, "We don't like to focus too much on young players – so many of them never pan out." To which I responded, "You're crazy if you don't let me do this story – I guarantee you that in five years this kid will be the best hockey player in the world."

"He's from where again?" they asked.

"Cole Harbour," I replied.

"Not exactly a hotbed, Bruce."

"Guys, you have to trust me."

Eventually, to their credit, they did.

I met Sidney face to face for the first time in December of 2001. Cameraman Eric Woolliscroft and I paid a visit to the Crosby family home on what would become a memorable Sunday afternoon. After meeting his parents, Trina and Troy, and his sister, Taylor, our next order of business became trying to figure out where to shoot some footage and interview Sidney. That mystery was instantly solved, however, when we saw the basement.

In one room, Troy had created a scaled-down, makeshift offensive zone, complete with red and blue lines on the concrete floor and a regulation-size net for Sidney to aim pucks at. About 10 feet or so behind the net and positioned off to the side was what has become arguably this country's most famous appliance: the Crosby family dryer (now on display, by the way, at the Nova Scotia Sport Hall of Fame). This poor thing was a total dog's breakfast, the victim of too many pucks shot with force, but just wide of the goal, by young Sidney. There were dials and buttons missing everywhere, and dents and black puck marks all over. Miraculously, though, it still worked. For the feature, we had Sidney fire puck after puck into the net, and then, with his last shot, deliberately miss and further add to the woes of the dryer. As the noise of puck on metal filled the house, the sheepish look on his face was priceless.

The family room made up the other part of the basement, and it was brimming with trophies and press clippings Sidney had accumulated in his still-blossoming hockey career. It provided the perfect backdrop for our all-important first interview with Sidney. As Eric focused the camera on Sidney's whiskerless face, I directed my first-ever question to the young man, and I remember it vividly...

"Sidney, when did you know, when did you first sense, that you were a better-than-average hockey player?"

In a voice that was still an octave or two away from full maturity, the answer came back with the mix of self-assurance and humility that would eventually define him...

"Well, I remember when I was in novice, I scored 169 goals in 20 games, and I realized then that I might have somewhat of a scoring touch."

Isn't that beautiful? By the way, one of Sidney's answers from this first-ever interview was used years later to punctuate a wonderfully produced Tim Horton's commercial. At the end of the ad, an adult Sidney is sitting in a dressing room. He begins to say "Wouldn't it be amazing, getting up every day," and then it cuts to fourteen-year-old Sidney finishing the sentence, "and playing, doing something that you love to do?" I can't help but smile every time I see it.

People often ask me what Sidney is really like, and my answer is always the same: just watch how he signs autographs, especially for kids. You can really see his true colours. So many professional athletes just scribble their names by rote, never looking up, never personalizing the experience for the fan. Sidney is the exact opposite – he always makes eye contact, always engages in a bit of conversation, and always goes out of his way to make sure a little kid leaves with a smile. *Duende*...

You wonder where this decency comes from only as it long as it takes for you to have a lengthy conversation with his parents. Trina and Troy are two of the most grounded, least demonstrative, least spotlight-seeking people you'd ever want to meet. They have rock-solid values and a real handle on what is truly essential in life. I know from an early age they taught Sidney that "please" and "thank you" were as fundamental as stickhandling and skating; that looking someone in the eye when having a conversation was as meaningful as an overtime goal; that remembering your sister's birthday was as important as any MVP award. Sidney learned these lessons well, and he's clearly never forgotten them. In every character-defining way, he's exactly the same today as he was before money and acclaim entered his life. That's quite a compliment to him and to his Mom and Dad.

Something else is worth noting about Sidney's parents. We live in an age where there are myriad stories of overbearing parents who pushed/forced their kids into a sport, and perhaps robbed them of some childhood along the way (tennis dads seem to be particular culprits). I can tell you unequivocally that Trina and Troy never pushed Sidney. If anything, he pushed them, so hard, in fact, that they were often extended beyond their financial means trying to keep up. Missed bill payments, extra jobs late at night, and remortgaging of the family home were facts of life for the Crosbys – all to make sure their son had good gear and the opportunity to travel to tournaments or attend camps in the summer. They afforded him every chance to follow his dream and fulfill the potential he showed at such a young age. But they never steered or forced him. In my opinion, that is parenting at its very pinnacle.

My most memorable experience with Sidney came in December of 2002, when Eric and I were dispatched by Hockey Night in Canada (the producers had become believers by then) to Faribault, Minnesota, where Sidney was spending his grade 10 year at a prep school called Shattuck St. Mary's. Shattuck had heavily recruited Sidney, wanting him to be the crown jewel in the school's renowned hockey program. Eric and I arrived to prepare a five-minute feature on Sidney to air on a future edition of Hockey Night in Canada.

We met up with Sidney, pinned a microphone on his shirt, and followed him to his first class, which was French. When it came his turn to speak, Sidney looked at the teacher and said, "Je suis Canadien!" As his classmates giggled, Sidney then spun in his seat to give a spirited thumbs-up to Eric's camera. Hey, it never hurts when the subject of your profile is a little bit of a ham.

After the school day ended, we headed to the small rink on campus to watch the Shattuck team practice. On the ice that day were future Buffalo Sabre Drew Stafford, future Tampa Bay Lightning Matt Smaby, and future Los Angeles King Jack Johnson. The squad was loaded, and would later go to win the US National Championship. Still, though, one player clearly stood out above the rest. I remember saying to Eric that day, "You know, if an alien landed right now from Mars and knew nothing about hockey, I bet you it would take him less than five minutes to pick out the best player on the ice." It was that obvious.

When practice ended, we walked with Sidney back to his dorm and prepared to say our goodbyes for the night. Before that could happen, though, Sidney asked, "What are you guys doing now?" I replied that we were probably going to drive to Bloomington, get some dinner, and then go visit the Mall of America. Seeing a wistful look suddenly fall over his face, I hesitantly followed with, "You wanna come with us?" The "yes" was out of his mouth faster than a speeding photon. So we all piled into our rented minivan and began what I remember to be about a forty-five-minute drive to Bloomington.

A spectacular Italian dinner preceded our visit to the second-biggest mall in North America. Eric went one way to do some shopping for his wife while Sidney and I went the other way just to browse around. We eventually came to a little cafe area, grabbed a couple of fruit smoothies, and sat for what I thought would be a minute or two. That minute quickly became an hour as we people-watched and talked. Eventually, as you would expect, the conversation drifted to sports. Sidney was fascinated as I told him stories of famous athletes and their intense drive. He was particularly transfixed by a bit of Michael Jordan lore...

In April of 1986, Jordan set an NBA playoff record by scoring 63 points in an overtime loss to the Boston Celtics. In that game, he went to the foul line 21 times, and made 19 of his free throws (a remarkable percentage). So despondent was he, though, at missing a couple that, the next morning, he was up at the crack of dawn and in the gym shooting baskets, a full three hours before his team was scheduled to practice. This after scoring 63 points and almost single-handedly beating what was then the best team in basketball.

Sidney digested this anecdote for a moment, looked down at his smoothie, paused, looked back up, and laid this one on me: "I guess it's no coincidence that the people who are best at what they do just happen to work the hardest." That pearl of wisdom from a fourteen-year-old kid in the food court of a mall. I've never forgotten it.

From my most memorable Sidney moment to my personal favourite...

In the chapter entitled "Boomer – *Poisson et Frites*," I tell the story of the March 2005 trip to Rimouski to watch Sidney play a couple of games in his final year of junior hockey. My Dad was on that trip, along with Boomer and his son, Brad. After the game

Hanging with Ron and Don during Hockey Day in Canada 2002.

First time on Hockey Night in Canada, first time in Air Canada Centre. Ken Dryden stopped by to wish me good luck. Surreal...

At the Shattuck-St.Mary's hockey rink in Minnesota with Sidney. He's just given me a keepsake.

One of my favourite pictures, taken in June of 2003 at Grand Parade Square in Halifax in front of the Cenotaph. From left – Kelly Hrudey, Sidney, CBC Cameraman Eric Woolliscroft, me, Scott Russell.

With Russ Anber in Athens, Greece, to cover Olympic Boxing for CBC in 2004.

With Catriona Le May Doan in Santo Domingo, Dominican Republic.
We were broadcasting the 2003 Pan Am Games, and became great pals.

My wedding party. From left – Lou LeBlanc, Boomer Gallant, Al MacLean, the Groom, Matt Rainnie, John MacIntosh, Mickey Fox. Check out Boomer's formal "footwear."

Kendra and I at our wedding reception. From the look on my face, you can tell who's approaching the podium to speak. That's right - Boomer!

With Hayley Wickenheiser, just moments after she led Canada to a gold medal
win over Sweden at the 2006 Olympics in Torino, Italy.

With Brad Gushue in Italy, moments after his gold medal victory over Finland in 2006.

With Sidney, rinkside in Montreal, prior to a matchup with the Canadiens. Able to elicit a smile...

With Rick Mercer and Boomer as we tape a snow-themed segment in Charlottetown for the "Rick Mercer Report."

With my Dad, Mark Rainnie, and Don Cherry on the set of "Coach's Corner."

Heather Moyse – an extraordinary person, and perhaps the single greatest athlete I've ever met.

On the set of "Compass" with Kendra, Mark, and my hockey hero, Guy Lafleur. Nobody has ever made me more nervous for an interview than "The Flower."

My two main little men, Mark (age 5 years) and Alistair (age 7 months). I love you guys so much!

on Saturday afternoon, Sidney and Troy met the four of us for dinner at the hotel restaurant. It was a great time, a chance for Sidney to let down his guard a bit and just kick back. No cameras, no microphones, no notepads – just six guys at a table laughing hard for two or three hours. The key point I'd like to make is that this was the first and only time my Dad had ever met Sidney and had the chance to talk to him. And he wouldn't see him again for another two years...

By that time, Sidney was the NHL's biggest star with the Pittsburgh Penguins. I was assigned to work a Penguins-Canadiens game in Montreal and, as a Christmas gift for my Dad, I arranged for him to accompany me and watch the game from the press box. On the morning of the game, the Penguins went through a quick practice and then returned to their dressing room to speak to media members. There must have been fifty, maybe even sixty reporters around Sidney's locker. I walked in with my Dad and we stood in the corner of the room just to watch what was going on. As we quietly observed the mayhem, there was suddenly a sliver of light between two reporters, and through that sliver, Sidney and I made fleeting eye contact. At that moment, he excused himself from further questions, stood up, and wove his way through the throng to where we were standing. Without hesitation, he extended his right hand to my Dad and said, "Mr. Rainnie, it's good to see you again." For Sidney, this was a full twenty-two months and maybe a million people after the dinner in Rimouski, and yet he remembered. You could have knocked my Dad over with a feather. That, my friends, is *duende*. Big time.*

---

*As I write this chapter, Sidney's hockey career is in limbo because of a brain injury he suffered in early 2010. A lot has already been written on the issue of concussions in hockey and it's light-years beyond my area of expertise.

I do, however, hope that Sidney reaches the point where he is safely able to play again, for the simple reason that he truly loves the game. Plus, when you're the best in the world at something, and you're just twenty-four years of age, it has to be excruciatingly hard to walk away. That being said, I also know that Sidney is too smart to do anything that would jeopardize his future or long-term health. I'm so glad he's getting the best advice possible and taking things slowly. You can be certain that whatever decision he settles on will be timely, informed, and made for all the right reasons. It's amazing that in a lifetime of being a role model, he is now becoming a shining example of how athletes should be extra cautious in returning from serious injury. Who knows – this might ultimately wind up being the most lasting part of his remarkable legacy.

Favourite Trivia Question #3

Muhammad Ali was never knocked out in his remarkable career, but he was knocked down three times. Which three fighters put him on the canvas?

GOLFING WITH THE FIDDLER

If you're familiar with the CBC Compass supper-hour program, then you are very familiar with Fred "The Fiddler" MacDonald. He is a man of such eminence that one nickname simply does not suffice. So, he also calls himself "The Sports Prophet," although no one is totally certain why, though there are rumours he has correctly predicted the outcome of a sporting event or two in his day. He comes from a large, storied, and extremely successful Charlottetown family. Fiddler is one of fourteen siblings and tells me he never actually slept alone until he got married. Fiddler is what we in the Maritimes call a "character." I absolutely love the guy, am proud to call him a friend, and am so glad he appears every Monday night on the show to share his unique insights.

His segment is called "The 5-Minute Flurry," and it generates as much response, both positive and negative, as anything we do. I think that's because Fred is such an excellent TV character: outspoken, occasionally outlandish, and always sporting a twinkle in his eye. He knows it's a show and realizes that people are tuning in not necessarily to be informed, but to be entertained. To that end, you never know what he's going to say, or if it has any chance of making sense. This all makes him prone to some of the finest moments of unintentional comedy that I've ever been witness to.

You want proof? Well, here are five actual gems he's unleashed on the Compass audience, taken verbatim from the program's transcripts. They are followed in parentheses by what I was actually thinking at the time. Here we go...

1) "New England will not win the game because they're not as well prepared as New England..." (Still, though, that would be quite a game!)

2) "I'm a prophet, not a genius. I never said I was Arthur Einstein!" (Albert's brother perhaps...)

3) "If history repeats itself, then we can probably expect the same thing to happen again." (Yes, we probably can...)

4) "I think if Montreal can score more goals, then they should win the game." (Keen insight there...)

5) Bruce: "Don't sit on the fence here, Fiddler. What do you think the chances are of Tiger Woods actually winning this Masters?"

Fiddler: "I think it's 50-50." (Thanks for not sitting on the fence!)

That last one is my personal favourite, and it almost sent me to the floor in fits of laughter. I can recall it took every ounce of strength for me to make it to the finish line of our segment that night...

I'd like to tell you about the one and only time Fiddler and I played golf together. And the story is not so much about the game, but instead the twenty-five-minute drive to the Avondale golf course.

I picked Fiddler up one sunny Thursday afternoon at the PEI Liquor Control Commission. This is where he "works," as Director of Marketing and Sales. His hours seem quite flexible. We piled his clubs into my car and off we went.

As we drove, Fiddler talked...and talked...and talked some more. I stared straight ahead, my eyes starting to glaze over and my brain beginning to actually hurt. Finally, though, he brought me into the discussion, as we started weighing the relative merits of team nicknames in professional sports.

We both agreed that "Yankees" is a great name and that "Red Sox" could be better. We disagreed on "Lightning" – I liked it, but Fiddler that day clearly preferred names that end with "s." For that reason, he also was sour on "Heat," "Magic," and "Wild." We debated hundreds of names and covered many kilometres when

I finally jumped in with this thought...

"You know what team has the most unimaginative, obvious, predictable nickname in any sport? The Peterborough Petes. I mean, how lazy and uninspired is that! The PETE-rborough Petes. That's brutal!"

"Yeah, that's pretty brutal," Fiddler agreed.

And then, trying to lighten the mood and make a little joke, I said, "Thank goodness that team isn't from Cochran, Alberta!"

Fiddler never cracked a smile and continued to stare straight ahead. Thinking he hadn't heard me, I reinforced my attempt at humour...

"COCH-ran, Alberta," I stressed.

Again, nothing from the passenger seat. After what seemed an uncomfortably long silence, Fiddler finally responded...

"You know, Bruce, I actually kind of like the Cochran Petes."

He's a beauty!

THE COMPLETE PACKAGE – HEATHER MOYSE

Late in 2010, I gathered with several colleagues at CBC PEI to discuss who should be named the province's Newsmaker of the Year. It turned out to be a fairly short meeting. Olympic Gold Medalist Heather Moyse was the runaway choice. Anytime you reach the podium on the grandest stage in sport, it's a remarkable thing. But when you do it in your home country, well, that's a whole different level of remarkable. For two magical nights in February of 2010, Heather Moyse and her bobsleigh partner, Kaillie Humphries, were the talk of not just the Vancouver Games, but of Canada as well. And the people of PEI watched every moment with a pride that united the Island from tip to tip.

As Newsmaker of the Year, Heather agreed to sit down for a 30-minute interview that aired on CBC in the last week of 2010. Incredibly, over a full year later, hardly a week goes by where someone doesn't approach me to tell me how much they enjoyed the one-on-one discussion with Heather. So I decided to go back and watch the interview again. I quickly discovered the lasting appeal had nothing to do with the interviewer, and everything to do with the interviewee! Heather was just so darn engaging. In particular, I found myself saying four things over and over again...

1) "Man, isn't she humble!" I found this particularly refreshing, given how such an alarming number of today's acclaimed athletes (especially well-paid professional athletes) are so smug or full of bluster.

2) "Wow, isn't she eloquent!" It is no surprise that she has become such an in-demand after-dinner speaker.

3) "What a wonderfully self-effacing sense of humour!" She actually has the timing of a good standup comic. It's not enough to be talented, attractive, and well-spoken, I guess...

4) "I think she's telling me things she's never told anyone else before." This is a good thing.

As I watched the interview from start to finish, I came to the obvious realization that Heather is far more capable of telling her Olympic story than I am. And what a story it is, with more plot twists than a good CSI episode, and subplots touching on themes like acceptance of others, turning negatives to positives, and daring to dream big. In fact, I think the best way to really meet Heather is to read a transcript of that interview. But, first, a little bit of context...

As Heather mentioned in her foreword to this book, she and I first met in December of 2005. I'm embarrassed to say, but at the time I knew surprisingly little about her. Oh sure, I had heard of her exploits as a young multi-sport star at Three Oaks High School in Summerside. I was also vaguely familiar with her outstanding track and field and rugby accomplishments at first the University of Waterloo and later the University of Toronto. And I was also aware that her name was all over a number of different PEI sports awards. But to say that I truly appreciated the extraordinary level of her talent at that time would be a stretch. It was only when I read that she had qualified for the Olympics just a few short weeks after being introduced to the sport of bobsleigh that my curiosity reached an apex. Was that even possible? Could that really be true? I had to meet her, and I had to make sure her journey was well-chronicled on our suppertime news program.

We were able to find a rare day that winter when she was actually home in Summerside with some time to spare. I followed her to the gym and watched her cruise through what to most would have been a life-ending workout. We then sat and talked in front of the camera. To say that Heather is a bit verbose is like saying that Boomer Gallant's shirts are a bit loud. In fact, she's the one person I've met that when you ask, "What time is it?" responds by giving you detailed instructions on how to build a watch. She claims to this day that I only asked three questions in thirty minutes of taping. In retrospect, I think it may have been two. Whatever the length of her answers, however, I can tell you that I was never bored listening. This is a testament to how engaging she is. Informative, too, especially when speaking of how her dominant attributes in rugby (speed and power) were directly transferrable to pushing a bobsleigh and getting it moving quickly. This correlation was fascinating to me. To help me tell this aspect of the story visually, I asked Heather if she had any footage of herself in rugby competition. After scouring her home, she was able to send me away with a DVD.

When I played the disc later that day back at CBC, I was stunned by what I saw. It was a game between the Canadian National Women's Rugby Team (Heather's squad) and the Scottish National Team. Now, I'm sure that every player on the field was world class, but there was only one who truly jumped from the screen. Heather was that dominant. She was running so fast that she almost looked like a character from a 1930s Keystone Cops film, where the action is sped up for comedic effect. Every other player looked to be stuck in quicksand as Heather flew by untouched, on her way to yet another try (a try is the equivalent of a touchdown in football – it's achieved by placing the ball on the ground behind the opponent's goal line). It was at this point I realized that I was dealing with one of the finest athletes I'd ever encountered. I also sensed that the sky was the limit for her in bobsleigh.

There, now, that should be sufficient context. Without further ado then, here is CBC PEI's 2010 Newsmaker of the Year Interview...

Bruce: "We could start this story pretty well anywhere and it would be good, but I thought it would be fun to ask you this: When was it and where were you when you first received a call from someone asking, 'Hey Heather, would you like to push a bobsled?'"

Heather: "I know exactly when that was, it feels like it was yesterday. It was May of 2001. I was sitting in my kitchen with my parents eating dinner and my Dad picked up the phone and he said, 'Heather it's for you,' and it was a track coach from the University of McGill, Dennis Barrett, and he just started saying, 'I used to be a bobsledder years ago, and Bobsleigh Canada has asked me to do recruiting in Eastern Canada and you're the first person, and really only person that came to mind. With your speed from sprinting and power with rugby, I thought you'd be perfect for it.' All of a sudden I said, 'Bobsledding,' and both of my parents, their heads just swiveled. And I said, 'Who does bobsledding?' That's all I could think of, and at the time I just turned it down. All I could think of was a uniform of Spandex from head to toe and that was just way too much Spandex for me!"

Bruce: "That was 2001, so you jump ahead to 2006, and we know you competed in Torino at the Olympics in Bobsled – what changed your mind from where it was in 2001?"

Heather: "Well one of the reasons I turned it down was I had already accepted a position to do some development work down in Trinidad and Tobago, so later in 2001, I went to Trinidad and was there for about three years. In the spring of '04, I moved to Toronto to do my master's degree, a two-year program. But after the first year, I went to my old track coach's retirement party, and that same recruiter happened to be there. He just kept nagging and nagging and saying, 'I think you should do this, I really think you should do this.' I finally said, 'FINE, just send me the information, we'll see when the training camps are and the testing, and I'll see if I can go.' And the next day I had a list of when they were coming to do testing in Toronto, and I just wrote back and said,

'Sorry, I've got rugby at that time, an international tournament with the national team, I guess it's not going to work out but it was really nice seeing you, thanks for calling.'

I suddenly ended up getting a phone call from the National Development Coach from Calgary, and he said, 'We received a message from Dennis Barrett that you can't come to our testing, but we think that you can bypass the testing and just come to our development camp.'"

Bruce: "They were very persistent."

Heather: "They were annoyingly persistent, actually. So I figured I'd go to the camp, but I thought it was a waste of time. I was in the middle of my master's and wasn't really keen. But I went, and ended up breaking a few of the testing records and then my mind as an athlete started to spin and I began wondering how well I could really do at this. And the fact that the Olympics – all of this was happening the last week of August/first week of September..."

Bruce: "The Olympics were five months away..."

Heather: "Right, and that just made it that much bigger of a challenge for me."

Bruce: "The history of sport is littered with athletes who either pick up a basketball and immediately sink the shot or pick up a baseball and throw a strike... Did you take to bobsleigh like that? Were you immediately really good at it?"

Heather: "Well, the first time down the track I threw up in my helmet. Seriously! But that aside, I was immediately pretty good. But it was just natural speed and power. I wasn't naturally good at the technique. If you listen to any footage, it's like, 'Oh, wow, too bad, she lost contact with the sled,' or 'Oooh, that technique is awful, but look, that's a start record!' People were always talking about my lack of technique, and I was such a new brakeman it was understandable, but then all of a sudden the start time would flash up and they'd be like, 'Well look at that – that's a new start record.'

Bruce: "Despite that ugly technique, we have a start record."

Heather: "Yeah, and some other countries started to come and video the starts and see how we were pushing and I was like, 'Sure, learn my terrible technique, go right ahead!'"

Bruce: "But here's the interesting thing, too – because you come in so late as a hotshot rookie from the sport of rugby, and you actually bump somebody from the team, don't you?"

Heather: (reluctantly) "Ahhh, yup."

Bruce: "And here's where the story really picks up, because the name of the person you end up bumping from the team is...??"

Heather: "Yeah, that person who had been working with Helen Upperton..."

Bruce: "Helen was the driver..."

Heather: "Yes. Working with Helen for over two years getting ready for the Olympics..."

Bruce: "Fully expecting to go to the Olympics..."

Heather: "Yes, going into the Olympic season as the number one brakeman on the team, her name was Kaillie Humphries."

Bruce: "I believe it still is!"

Heather: (laughing) "Yes, I don't think she's entered any witness protection program!"

Bruce: "So you come in, like I say this rugby hotshot, and Kaillie all of a sudden isn't going to push the bobsleigh for Helen Upperton at the Games in Torino, you are..."

Heather: "Yes."

Bruce: "Well you can just imagine the hard feelings. Let's put that aside for a moment and jump to those games. You and Helen Upperton go..."

Heather: "As serious medal contenders..."

Bruce: "Right, and how close do you get to winning a medal in Italy, if people don't remember?"

Heather: "Yeah, this was the only race that Helen and I did together that year where we didn't win a medal, and we missed the podium by five one-hundredths of a second."

Bruce: "So after four runs you add up the times..."

Heather: "After four runs which equals 5.7 kilometres of track, five one-hundredths of a second."

Bruce: "Your Dad's a doctor – what is that equivalent too, five one-hundredths of a second?"

Heather: "We tried to look this up actually... An accelerated heart-rate during intense exercise is actually half a second, five-tenths of a second. A blink of an eye, everyone thinks that's so fast, well that's actually three-tenths of a second. The closest thing we could equate it to so people could really understand was the single beat of a hummingbird's wing, and that is actually still more than five one-hundredths – it's actually between ten and fifteen one-hundredths."

Bruce: "So you miss a medal by that amount?"

Heather: "Yup."

Bruce: "So after Torino, you have a choice to make. You have to decide if you want to hang around this sport for four more years and try it again, or do you want to do something else with life? That's your decision?"

Heather: "Well, my decision from the very beginning had been, 'OK, I've got five months to do this and then I'm going back to finish school.' So my priority was to finish my master's degree. One, I had never considered sport to be a career, I had always considered it to be extracurricular, for fun, on the side, if I could fit it in with whatever I was doing for a living. I grew up in an academic family, and I grew up in PEI. I mean, nobody around here was training for the Olympics. You don't see someone at the local gym that you can tangibly point to and say, 'Oh that person is going to the Olympics in luge, or biathlon, or skeleton...'"

Bruce: "Or bobsleigh."

Heather: "Or bobsleigh."

Bruce: "I am guessing that for someone as competitive as you, you had a tough time being that close to what is Olympic glory."

Heather: "Yes, it was very difficult, it was frustrating certainly at the time, but the hardest thing was later when you got home and you realized just how close it was, that's really tough, the only race that we did not win a medal in just happened to be the only one that the world cared about. Nobody cared about the World Cup races. It was really tough – it kept nagging at me all year, it was like unfinished business, and I had to go back."

Bruce: "After the Olympics, you took a bit of time off, and in that time your driver, Helen Upperton, found another partner she liked. So when you came back, you had to find another driver. And here's where the plot really thickens, because the driver you were paired with next was…??"

Heather: "Kaillie Humphries."

Bruce: "The same Kaillie Humphries who was once a pusher and was unceremoniously bumped from the team by Heather Moyse."

Heather: "Well, see, this is the thing. When she started driving, she actually had a ton of potential right away. She was so strong. Her driving skills were not consistent, but they showed a lot of potential. And this all seems like a fairy tale, like we just kind of fit together – I needed a driver, she's now driving. But in the fall of 2008 when I came back, we STILL WEREN'T TALKING! We were just kind of living our lives simultaneously in the sport…"

Bruce: "You were far from friends at this point?"

Heather: "We were SO far from friends. We were very reluctant teammates. And then, as fate would have it, we were put in the same van on a road trip. Now road trips in bobsleigh are far from glamorous. They can be anywhere from five hours to eleven hours driving between European countries for various races. So we were stuck on this long road-trip. So we do everything to try to pass the time – we talk about boys, we talk about other teammates, we talk about family from home, we try to tell jokes – just anything to pass the time. Now I had been given by a friend of mine what's called an 'If' book. It's full of a thousand questions like, 'If you could have dinner with any three people dead or alive, who would they be and why?' Just a ton of questions like that. So I'm in the back seat reading this book and just kind of rattling off scenarios and all of a sudden I come across this question, 'If you could get back at someone who wronged you in the past, who would it be?' And my voice sort of trailed off and it was so awkward. And the van was just SO quiet. I tried to make light of the situation and make a joke, and I said, 'Haaa, haaa, I'm probably in your top ten, aren't I, Kaillie?' And she just paused, which made it even more awkward, and she said, 'No, actually you're not. I've come to realize that you were just doing your job and doing what you needed to do. It wasn't you that made the situation difficult and strained the way it was – it actually had nothing to do with you.' Now, I had no idea how much weight I had been carrying on my shoulders and I just kind of felt it lift. And it was perfect, because less than a month later, we became a permanent team. It was perfect because now I had a way to give back to her after feeling I had taken something from her."

Bruce: "I always thought, too, that here she was, one of the best pushers in the world until you came along. Then you come in, and you quickly become the best pusher in the world. Both of you pushing the sled – that must be tremendous acceleration at the top of the hill."

Heather: "It is. Kaillie is stronger than I am, but I'm faster than she is, which makes a perfect combination at the top. The power of both of us together get it going so fast at the beginning and then once we reach the crest of the hill, she can get in and I can take a few extra steps before getting in to accelerate the sled and get the best velocity. It's not just about start time, it's about start time and then the velocity of sending the sled shooting into the track."

Bruce: "You're like the ultimate team."

Heather: (laughs) "It's been a good combination!"

Bruce: "I would say. So you get to Whistler and you just don't win gold, you just obliterate the competition. And I know that for two nights this Island's attention was focused on the TV, and I think we even bumped a Canada-Russia hockey game to see how Heather was going to do. Did you know how well you were doing and where you stood, because you were breaking track records every time you came down?"

Heather: "We actually had no idea. Finally at the Olympic Games I convinced Kaillie to not look at any of our times. We knew what our starts were like, and we also knew where we were sitting. We knew we were sitting in first after the first run because we were going last in the second run, and you go in reverse order of finish. But we had no idea how far ahead we were of the next team. We didn't know if that team was one-hundredth of a second behind us – we could have been almost tied for what we knew. And we left it like that, so that each individual heat would be treated separately and we would just do our best for that heat. And we knew if we won each individual heat, then we would ultimately win the whole thing."

Bruce: "You must have known doing this as often as you had that this was feeling right..."

Heather: "It felt great. Kaillie was on fire with some of her runs. If you watch the last heat, though, we knew we were ahead, but coming out of the first corner there's a little straight stretch before the second corner, and I knew we fishtailed – we kind of skidded going through there. Kaillie hates it, because that's the run that everybody shows. But that was scary, because whenever you fishtail you slow way down, and we could have lost all the time we had built up from our start, and the advantage we had from our start could have been all lost right there. In the back I had no idea, but I was like, 'Get it together, Kaillie, get it together.' Sometimes a fishtail like that rattles a driver and the rest of the ride is all bumpy, but to Kaillie's credit, she held it together and we got it done. It's crazy if you could hear the things going on in my head. As you go, you can feel the sled picking up speed, you can feel coming out of the corners the whooshes and the g-forces, and it just felt SO RIGHT, and in my head I'm saying, 'Yes, Kaillie, faster, good job, good job,' and you just feel the speed building and building, and it's just perfect."

Bruce: "It's so neat that the two of you, once so at odds, made history together."

Heather: "And we're best of friends now."

Bruce: "For everybody who will never get the chance to stand with a gold medal and watch the Canadian flag rise while the national anthem is being played, what's a word or two to describe what that is like?"

Heather: (pause, eyes fill up) "Overwhelming. Emotional. And now it feels very surreal. Sometimes it actually seems like it never happened."

Bruce: "Well perspective's a weird thing because it was ten months ago, and I can only assume that sometimes it feels like yesterday, and some days it must feel like forever ago."

Heather: "There was such a build-up, it was such a long wait to 2010, even now when people mention 2010, I still get the butterflies and anxiety, because 2010 for me was the Olympics. It was the thing I had worked so hard to get ready for. It was the moment I had waited four long years for."

Bruce: "OK – where are you now, and where will you be in the next year regarding sport?"

Heather: "I'm currently on the injury list. I demolished my ankle playing in the last game of the Rugby World Cup in September, and I've just started running within the last week or so and I'm planning on competing again with the Bobsled team in January in Europe."

Bruce: "You're gonna push the sled again for Kaillie Humphries?"

Heather: "Try to push her as well as last year and finish off the season with Kaillie."

Bruce: "Final one for you – 2014 Winter Olympic Games in Russia, is it on your radar at all?"

Heather: "It's on Kaillie's! (laughs) But I'm taking things one year at a time. I have no idea. I have no idea what I'm doing next year or the year after. As long as I'm where I want to be each individual year, and as long as each year presents challenges and chances to grow, then I'll be happy and life will be good."

Bruce: "Well that's a good spot to be. Congratulations again on a magnificent accomplishment, and thanks for being here."

Heather: "Thank you!!"

A few months after winning Olympic Gold in Vancouver, Heather was back on the rugby pitch, leading Canada at the 2010 Women's Rugby World Cup in England. Late in the tournament, she was tackled awkwardly and severely injured her ankle. Despite this, she still led the tournament in tries with seven.

So to recap – in 2010, Heather was BEST IN THE WORLD in her winter sport and BEST IN THE WORLD in her summer sport. And who was named Canada's female athlete of the year? Not Heather, but figure skater Joannie Rochette, who won a bronze medal at the Olympics in Vancouver. I may be biased, but does that sound right to you?

You should also know that Heather was able to recover sufficiently from her ankle injury to push the sled for Kaillie in February of 2011 at the World Bobsleigh Championships in Germany. And even though she was far from 100 per cent, she was still able to help write another chapter of Canadian sport history. The team of Moyse and Humphries won bronze, becoming the first Canadian women's duo ever to win a medal at a bobsleigh world championship.

As I write this, Heather is fully engaged in yet another major athletic challenge. In June of 2011, with her ankle still not quite right, she went looking for a new, low-impact way to maintain the speed and power in her legs. She found that cycling was the answer. She also found, not surprisingly, that she was really good at it. Her goal now: to qualify for the National Track Cycling Team and race for Canada in the 2011–2012 season. Seriously, are you going to bet against her? And if you are, give me a call. I'll gladly take the bet.

BOOMER – CALLS TO TORINO

The thing about great sports or political events is that they are dramas without a script. That's why they are so challenging and fun to cover for a broadcaster. Anything can happen. We know what we might expect will happen, but we never know for sure. And you might see something truly dramatic, or you might see something you've never seen before. So there is always that sense of anticipation before a big event.

Never was that sense higher for me than before the 2006 Olympic Games in Torino, Italy. These were the Winter Olympics, and I was given what had the potential to be a dream dual assignment. I would be the play-by-play announcer for women's hockey and the rink-side reporter for curling. For a Canadian broadcaster, nothing beats the thrill of describing a gold medal performance by a Canadian athlete or team. And here I was directly involved in two sports that were likely to yield golden results for Canada.

Let's talk first about the curling. The event was held in a gorgeous little town called Pinerolo, about 40 kilometres southwest of Torino. Canada was represented on the women's side by the Shannon Kleibrink rink from Alberta and on the men's side by the Brad Gushue rink from Newfoundland and Labrador. The Kleibrink team never really found its groove at these Games, but still managed to play well enough to win a bronze medal. The Gushue rink was a different story entirely. This foursome got off to a very slow start, but gradually improved as the week rolled along. By the medal round they were smoking hot, and, by the gold medal game, darn near unstoppable. Team Canada totally outclassed Finland in the championship game, but the play on the ice was really only a subplot. You might recall the touching story involving the young skip of this team. As 25-year-old Brad

Gushue curled in Italy, his mom, Maureen, watched from New-foundland, unable to attend because of her exhausting battle with bowel cancer (a battle she would eventually win). I was standing 15 feet from the rings when the final stone was thrown, and, in the bedlam that ensued, watched as Brad was handed a cell phone. CBC cameras zeroed right in and clearly picked up Brad saying, "Come on, Mom, answer, answer!!" She did, and his excitement as he spoke to his biggest fan touched everyone that was watch-ing. They talked for maybe a minute, and then Brad headed my way for his first interview as a gold medalist. I could tell he was on the verge of breaking down, so I kept it simple by saying, "Give us a sense of what this means to you."

He tried to respond, but words just wouldn't come. Tears did, though, and he wound up burying his face in his hands. When he emerged, maybe 15 seconds later, he looked at me with red in his eyes and apologized, saying, "I'm sorry I'm such a sook!"

All I could think of to utter in response was, "Don't be silly and don't apologize. You're the farthest thing in the world from a sook." He laughed a little and, at that moment, I saw him relax. I then went where I would never have gone just mere moments earlier. I asked, "Without sharing anything too personal, can you give us a sense of what was just said on the telephone between you and your Mom?"

He looked at me, took a deep breath, smiled, and said, "I just told her I loved her."

For obvious reasons, this interview remains one of the truly honest and special moments of my career. Brad and I remain good friends to this day, and I'll always be thankful I was there to greet him in Pinerolo.

Let's move to women's hockey. As I mentioned earlier, I was assigned play-by-play duties for this event. What a challenge this was! I had never really done hockey play-by-play before, and here, now, on the biggest stage in the world, I was about to sink or swim.

It really is a daunting task – you have to learn the names, pronunciations, numbers, positions, ages, and hobbies of approximately 200 female hockey players (8 teams, 24 players per team), and you have to fit each player instantly into the flow of the game. The best in the business (Jim Hughson, Bob Cole, Chris Cuthbert) do this with seamless ease. I was, and remain, far from this category. Still, I prepared well. I did my research, and felt ready to go. Before the first game, I remember coming up with a mission statement that would carry me through the week to come. I told myself, "You're going to make mistakes, but just keep going. People watching at home probably won't even notice and, if they do, they'll understand."

That was my mindset as I readied for a game between Canada and Russia. Early in the second period, I commented on the Russian goaltender, who was playing much better than she had in the first. Trying to convey this, I chimed in with this beauty: "Gashennikova has really picked it up here in the second. She's done a complete 360!" I realized right away that my calculations would put her back exactly where she started, and that the degree reading I was actually looking for was 180. But instead of drawing attention to the error, I decided instead to forge on, hoping that no viewer had picked up the mathematical anomaly.

That night in my hotel room, I sat preparing for the next day's game. It was about midnight Torino time when my cell phone unexpectedly rang.

"Hello," I said.

"Hello, I'm looking for Bruce Rainnie," came a voice that sounded poorly disguised and vaguely familiar.

"This is Bruce."

"Bruce, this is Dick Ebersol, President of NBC Sports calling."

"Yes, sir," I hesitantly replied.

"Listen, I saw your work on the hockey game tonight, and am

interested in offering you a job."

"Really?"

"Absolutely. To be honest, I wasn't impressed by your work in the first period, but by the end of the game I thought you were great! You might say, I did a complete 360!!"

At that point, it hit me like a Tyson right to the jaw. "Boomer, go to bed, and don't call me anymore!"

The next day, Canada took on Sweden, and I talked myself smack into another predicament. The Swedes had a woman who played defence in a manner that reminded me of former Toronto Maple Leaf great, Borje Salming. Her name was Joa Elfberg, and she even wore number 21, which was the same number Salming wore during his NHL career. In my attempt to point this out, something went horribly wrong. This is my actual commentary from the second period of this game:

"Elfberg with the puck for Sweden, winding up behind her net. You know, you watch her play, and you can't help but notice – she's got a lot of Salami in her!"

Again, I told myself, "Just keep going. It happened so quickly it's highly unlikely that anybody noticed anyway."

Later that night, back in my hotel room, I'm studying notes for future matchup. Just as I'm about to turn in for the night, you guessed it, my cell phone rang...

"Hello," I said.

"Heeelllloooo," a seemingly older voice responds, struggling to get the word out.

"Yes, hello."

"Is this Bruce Rainnie?"

"Yes."

"Mr. Rainnie, this is Charlie from 'Charlie's Delicatessen' back here in Charlottetown."

"Yes..."

"Listen, I know you'll be traveling home soon. I was wondering if you could bring me back some of that Borje Salami?"

"Boomer, put the phone down and GO TO BED!!"

The gold medal game finally arrives, and it's a rematch between Canada and Sweden. The Canadians dominate the game, and from a broadcast perspective, I have my most consistent performance of the week. Nothing spectacular, mind you, but also nothing that sticks out like a sore thumb. I do, however, close the game with a line that is a wee bit cheesy. As the time ticks to zero, I bellow into my microphone, "Yet another work of art in Italy, this one a Canadian masterpiece!" I figure this is just corny enough to warrant another phone call.

That night, I sit in my room, and stare in anticipation at my cell phone. I know what's coming and, truth be told, am a little disappointed when minutes and then hours pass by. I'm about to give up hope when, as though on cue, the ring comes. This time, I'm ready...

"Hello."

"Yes, I'm looking for Bruce Rainnie?" The voice this time is unusually rich and resonant. Clearly, I figure, another fake...

"This is Bruce," I sharply reply.

"Bruce, this is Peter Mansbridge calling from 'The National' back in Toronto. On behalf of everyone who watched that game, I just wanted to tell you what a fine job you did broadcasting this golden moment back to all of us here in Canada. Fine job, young man, you should be very proud!"

At this point, I've heard enough. "Boomer, kiss my arse!" (Or words to that effect...)

From the other end of the line comes silence. And then, after an agonizing few seconds, this question...

"What the heck did you say?"

"I said, 'Kiss my arse!'"

"That's what I thought you said. Why? What's your problem?"

The voice still sounds remarkably deep and profound. In fact, it continues to sound remarkably like Peter Mansbridge's voice.

"Who is this really?" I anxiously ask.

"I already told you, it's Peter Mansbridge calling from 'The National.' Who did you think it was?"

I figure now is the time to come clean: "I thought it was Boomer playing another one of his jokes. I'm really sorry, Mr. Mansbridge. I really am."

Again, an excruciating silence. Finally, Peter Mansbridge, host of 'The National,' utters words that are magic to my ears...

"This involves Boomer – Boomer Gallant?"

"Yes," I meekly reply.

"Bruce, stop apologizing right now. I don't blame you for this. I've met Boomer and I know Boomer. You have my sympathies!"

Favourite Trivia Question #4

Name the NHL rookies who have scored 100 or more points in their rookie seasons.

MY THREE ALL-TIME FAVOURITE CALLS IN SPORTS BROADCASTING...

1) Game 7 of the 1988 Eastern Conference semifinals between Atlanta and Boston, and Larry Bird and Dominique Wilkins engage in a duel for the ages. Wilkins scores 47 points, but Bird scores 20 in the fourth quarter, including two on a left-handed lay-up with 26 seconds left. With Boston Garden going crazy, Brent Musburger of CBS intones, "You are watching what greatness is all about!" Spine-tingling.

2) Dan Kelly calling game three of the best hockey series ever played, the 1987 Canada Cup final between Canada and the Soviet Union. The score was tied 5-5, the faceoff was deep in the Canadian end, and the play began to head up ice...

"Lemieux ahead to Gretzky, has Murphy with him on a two-on-one. To Lemieux. In on goal. He shoots! HE SCORES!! Mario Lemieux with 1:26 remaining!"

Every Canadian who watched this game can remember exactly where they were. I was in my basement with my late uncle, Bob, and when Lemieux scored, we screamed so loud the walls shook.

3) 1996 in Atlanta. Donovan Bailey had already won the men's 100 metre final, and he was now anchoring Team Canada in the 4 by 100 metre relay. As he sprinted to the finish line with a sizable lead, the late Don Wittman captured the moment perfectly.

"Oh, if you're Canadian you have to love Saturday nights in Georgia."

Maybe his best line in a career that was full of so many.

"GOLD! CANADA! IGALI!"

Probably the best phone call I've ever received in my broadcasting career came in the spring of 2000. On the other end of the line was Joel Darling, a well-known and distinguished producer for CBC Sports in Toronto. I had been on Joel's radar for some time, and he had assured me that if he were ever fronting a network production "out east," he would offer me the chance to work on it. I had been waiting what seemed an eternity for the phone to ring...

"Hi Bruce, this is Joel Darling," he said.

"Hi Joel," I replied, trying to sound cool and collected.

"Quick question for you."

"Sure, go ahead."

"How would you like to go to Sydney?" he asked.

Not being much of world traveler by this point in my career, I innocently answered, "I'd love to! But what's going on in Cape Breton?"

Silence at the other end of the line, followed by stifled laughter. After a moment, Joel continued...

"Bruce, I'm the Executive Producer of CBC's Olympic Coverage this summer in Sydney – Sydney, Australia, that is. And I'm wondering if you'd like to be part of my broadcast team?"

I don't remember exactly how I responded at this point, but I'm sure it was with something clever and understated like, "ABSO-FREAKIN'-LUTELY!!" My mind was instantly racing, and, in a flash, I thought of all the summer sports he might ask me to cover. Would it be track and field, basketball (my personal favourite), boxing, tennis (also a favourite), maybe even baseball or softball?

Joel continued, "Excellent. So, you'll be heading to Australia to work on what could be the best Olympics ever. And among a group of commentators I consider to be the most skilled in the world, I have full confidence that you can hold your own."

"Thanks so much, Joel," I replied. "I'll do my best to reward that confidence."

And then, unable to harness my curiosity any longer, I sort of blurted, "So, what will I be doing?"

"Well," he said, getting right to the point, "what do you know about weightlifting and wrestling?"

"Not too much," I said, a bit stunned.

"Well, you have three months to become an expert!"

And with that, my first Olympic experience began.

For the next 12 weeks, I studied as hard as I ever did for any university exam I ever took. As a matter of fact, because I was covering two sports, it was almost like studying for two exams. I'm talking three to four hours a day, reading books, watching tape, talking to coaches – basically immersing myself. By the time the Games rolled around, I knew every nuance of both disciplines: the origins, the evolutions, the rules, the legendary figures, and the contemporary greats. I felt as polished as possible. And then the Olympics began...

Weightlifting was first on the schedule, and I quickly came to the realization that I would not get to share much of the information I had accumulated in my studies. That's because the bloody lifts happen so fast. Basically a guy walks out, takes a couple of deep breaths, and tries to lift a really heavy bar. Months and months of research, binders full of notes and stats, my head swimming with biographical information, and all I have time to say is one of two things...

1) "He lifted it!" or

2) "Oh, too bad! He's not able to lift it."

Ten straight days of weightlifting competition, and I basically exhausted slightly differing variations of the above two options. I also learned something quite interesting about CBC's coverage of the Olympic Games. I learned that if you're covering a sport in which Canadians aren't doing well, you aren't going to get much air time. And when you do, it is not likely to come during the prime time hours. Canada is not an international weightlifting power. So, suffice to say, I'm sure many of you don't have vivid recollections of hearing my insightful commentary from Sydney. Freestyle wrestling, however, proved to be a much different story, all thanks to a marvelous athlete by the name of Daniel Igali.

Daniel was born and raised in the village of Eniwari in Bayelsa State in southeastern Nigeria. His father was an accountant, and thank goodness for that, because only a man in command of numbers could keep track of a family that included four wives and twenty-one children. So Daniel basically grew up wrestling – for the softest spot in the bunk beds, for the most appetizing plate of supper, for the prime spot in the line to the bathroom. Regarding the size of his family, he told me once during an interview that "if you include the wives, we have enough for two football teams, and reserves!"

He came to Victoria, BC, in 1994 to wrestle for Nigeria at the Commonwealth Games. He was full of potential but wasn't very good at the time, finishing 11th in the competition. After the Games, he made the biggest decision of his young life. Because of the overwhelming political unrest in his country, he chose to stay in Canada and to become a citizen. His wrestling career blossomed under Canadian coaching, and by 1999, he was World Champion in the 69 kg (152 lb) weight class – the first Canadian ever to win a wrestling world championship. He entered the 2000 Olympics in Sydney as a strong favourite to further break new ground and win Canada's first-ever gold medal in wrestling.

A few of his early matches very agonizingly close, much closer than expected, in fact, and we all wondered if Igali was being overwhelmed by the pressure to win gold. We later learned that he was wrestling with a fairly serious knee injury, a fact he chose to keep between himself and his coaches. Still, though, he moved on, and entered the final day of the 2000 Olympics needing to win two more matches...

Remember, now, these games had not been particularly successful for Canada. (Summer Games rarely are – for obvious climate-related reasons, Canadians generally fare much better in Winter Olympics.) As we went to air that morning, Canada had won only two gold medals at the 2000 Olympics. Simon Whitfield, the triathlete, had won the first. And the Canadian men's tennis doubles team of Daniel Nestor and Sébastien Lareau had won the second. So, all eyes (about eight million of them) were on Daniel Igali, and by extension on me, as well. I didn't want to drop the ball...

In the semifinal, he faced a tough American by the name of Lincoln McIlravy. Igali had beaten McIlravy at the 1999 World Championships, and to say there was no love lost between the two would be an understatement.

Igali trailed 3-2 late in the match, tied the score with only 12 seconds left in regulation time, then won in dramatic fashion in what proved to be a tantalizing overtime session. As he reached to shake McIravy's hand, the American pushed it away in disgust. Later, McIlravy would whisper in Igali's ear, "You're the best I've ever seen" (this is all on YouTube if you ever have the urge to check it out). Igali was off to the gold medal match, to be held about three hours later.

I realized that most of Canada would be watching Igali wrestle for gold, and I also realized that this could be my big break. I just knew Igali was going to win – he had come too far to do anything but. It was my chance to now make some broadcast history – to punctuate his victory with words that would forever accompany what would be enduring video. Now, normally, I try not to write anything down. As a rule, I prefer the words to come naturally, unscripted, from the heart. But this moment was too big, and I was too damn nervous. I needed something to have in my hand that I could refer to at Igali's moment of victory. So, I went outside the arena, ordered a cheeseburger at a great little cafe, took out an index card, and began to write...

"Like his hero Martin Luther King, Daniel Igali had a dream. And that dream has come to fruition on the shimmering shores of Sydney Harbour." Good stuff, I thought. I would then pause, let the words sink in, and finish with this flourish...

"From the humblest of beginnings to the loftiest of conclusions, his story is one to inspire, his story is so uniquely Canadian."

There, I had it! Total cheese, but it sounded good. I'd start the soliloquy with about 10 seconds left in the match, and then hit my final word just as the final bell was rung. Man, was I ready...

The opponent in the final was Arsen Gitinov of Russia, and although a good wrestler, he was nowhere near Igali's class. Sure enough, as time began to tick down, Igali was in full control with an insurmountable lead. With about 15 seconds left and excitement reaching a crescendo, I stood up and pulled the index card from my suit pocket. My broadcast partner, a former Canadian wrestler by the name of Chris Wilson, also stood, and started moving his hands wildly in anticipation. Sure enough, his big mitt hit my right elbow bang on the ulnar nerve (better known as the "funny bone"), and forced the involuntary release of the card from my hand. In slow motion, I watched the card fall to the floor while time began to tick down. My eyes began shifting, from card in free fall to the arena's time clock (six, five, four, three...). Sensing that the moment was about to pass and desperate for my piece of broadcast immortality, I hesitantly cried out with the only three words that would come to mind...

"Gold!" (uncomfortable pause)

"Canada!" (more discomfort)

"Igali!"

(You can also see these final moments on YouTube, although I urge you not to rush to do so...)

And just like that, it was over. Igali's hand was being raised, and I was certain of two things...

1) I had just witnessed a superior athlete create one of the defining moments in Canadian Olympic history, and

2) I would never work for CBC Sports again.

Years later, I'm pleased to say that, like many things in life, it seemed worse at the time than it actually was. And, ultimately, it didn't prove career-limiting in any way. In fact, I shudder now to think of how my original plan might have unfolded. In particular, I'm terrified to think that I was fully ready to unleash words like "shimmering" and "fruition" on an unsuspecting audience. Thank you, fate (and ulnar nerve), for jumping in when you did.

There's an interesting footnote to this story. About three months after the Olympics, I was home one day when the doorbell rang. It was a guy from Purolator Courier, and he was delivering a rather substantial package.

I opened it, and found a limited-edition framed lithograph of Daniel Igali winning his gold medal in Sydney. And when I checked the return address, I was shocked to discover it had been sent to me by Daniel himself. On the back of the picture, he wrote the following...

"Dear Bruce – thanks for playing such a big role in one of the biggest days of my life. Every time I watch the tape, I get goose bumps when you say 'Gold! Canada! Igali!' It's just so perfect!"

Great athlete, great taste. Isn't it funny how things work out?

ATHLETES I WISH I HAD SEEN IN THEIR ABSOLUTE PRIMES

Muhammad Ali

On February 25, 1964, he beat Sonny Liston and won the heavy-weight title for the first time. On March 22, 1967, he beat Zora Folley in his last fight before being stripped of the title for refusing induction into the US Army. During that three-year, one-month stretch, he fought 10 times, and just might have been the greatest athlete who ever lived. For a big man (and he was MUCH bigger than most people remember, standing 6'3" tall and weighing 215 pounds), he had the grace of a gazelle and the stamina of a marathon runner. He was perfectly proportioned, with long legs and arms, smallish waist, and powerful shoulders. The speed in both his hands and feet were such that he could hit an opponent 10 to 15 times and then be well out of range by the time a counterpunch was thrown. Combine these natural physical gifts with a not-so-quiet confidence and you had a package of irresistible magnetism.

What I wouldn't give to have been front row for those 10 fights, especially the ones with Jimmy Ellis, Floyd Patterson, Cleveland Williams, and Ernie Terrell.

Bobby Orr

I really only remember seeing Bobby Orr play during the 1976 Canada Cup. He was named MVP of the tournament and was more often than not the best player on the ice, despite playing on basically one healthy leg (repeated injuries had essentially destroyed his left knee by this point). His career pretty much ended with that series (he would go on to play only 26 more NHL games). The DVD *The Best of Bobby Orr* is one of my favourites, and I highly recommend it. It shows virtually all of the goals Orr scored in his career, 270 in the regular season, another 26 in the playoffs. As you watch this DVD, you find yourself saying, over and over, "That was the best goal I've ever seen." It would have been something to see Bobby in the 1970–71 season in particular. That year, he became the first player to post more than 100 assists in a season. And for the year, he was a staggering plus 124! All of that at age twenty-two. I have to agree with Mr. Cherry when he says that Orr is the greatest ever to play the game.

Sandy Koufax

The last five years of Sandy Koufax's career are transcendent, unparalleled in baseball history. He was a threat to throw a no-hitter literally every time he took to the mound. And when the games mattered most, he found yet another gear. In eight career starts in the World Series, his ERA was an almost unthinkable 0.95.

Arthritis forced him to retire at age thirty, in the very heart of his prime. In his final year, he won 27 games and posted an ERA of 1.73. He is one of a select few athletes ever to walk away at the very top of his/her game (Jim Brown, Barry Sanders, Rocky Marciano, Annika Sorenstam, Bjorn Borg, and Ken Dryden are others who spring to mind).

Pete Maravich

He averaged 44.2 points a game for his four-year university career at Louisiana State University, even though every opponent knew he was taking virtually every shot. Basketball historians have gone back to check the video archives, and many surmise that had the 3-point line been in existence, Maravich's average would have been closer to 54 or 55 points a game. Plus, he was a tremendous showman. Behind-the-back passes, between-the-legs dribbling, shots taken while off-balance or on the run – you'd see it all when you saw Maravich play.

Bob Gibson

In three World Series with the Cardinals, his record was 7 and 2, with a 1.89 ERA, and eight complete games... MVP of both the 1964 and 1968 World Series... The most intimidating pitcher of the last fifty years, and arguably the fiercest competitor ever to play major league baseball. His former catcher, and current TV analyst Tim McCarver, once said, "Bob Gibson is the luckiest pitcher I ever saw. He always pitches when the other team doesn't score any runs."

Ted Williams

He batted .388 as a thirty-eight-year-old, and hit a very respectable .316 his final season as a forty-two-year-old. Plus, he homered in his last-ever at bat. Consider that he hit 521 career home runs while missing nearly five prime years because he was serving in the Second World War and the Korean War. He once said, "A man has to have goals – for a day, for a lifetime – and that was mine, to have people say, 'There goes Ted Williams, the greatest hitter who ever lived.'" Most baseball historians would say he achieved his goal.

Joe Dimaggio

The 56-game hitting streak is one thing, but consider another stat, which I would argue is equally as impressive... Joe Dimaggio hit 361 career home runs (that number would have been much higher, but Yankee Stadium was cavernous for right-handed hitters in Dimaggio's day), and struck out ONLY 369 times. By comparison, Willie Mays struck out 1,526 times, Mickey Mantle 1,710 times, Babe Ruth 1,330 times, and even Ted Williams struck out 709 times.

Dimaggio must have been something. *The New York Times* said in an editorial when he retired, "The combination of proficiency and exquisite grace which Joe DiMaggio brought to the art of playing center field was something no baseball averages can measure and that must be seen to be believed and appreciated."

Jim Brown

He played nine NFL seasons, and led the league in rushing eight times. His career average of 5.2 yards per carry is by far the best in football history. And he never missed a game, despite being the most physical, punishing runner of his era. This is a player who loved to initiate contact, and never ran out of bounds to avoid a hit.

His success as a multi-sport athlete while at Syracuse University is mind-boggling. In addition to his football accomplishments, he excelled in basketball, track, and especially lacrosse. In fact, many who watched him play think that with his speed and power, he might have been the greatest lacrosse player who ever lived. In his senior year, he was named a first-team All-American, scoring a remarkable 43 goals in just 10 games.

Bobby Hull

The first player to score more than 50 goals in a season... Famous for his end-to-end rushes at Chicago Stadium, many of which culminated with a 110 mph slapshot just inside the opposition blueline... Pound for pound, maybe the strongest player ever to play professional hockey.

Jack Nicklaus

He burst on the golf scene in the early 1960s – a player with huge legs and tremendous strength. He ushered in the power era in golf, as he was able to bash 300-yard drives with the tiny little persimmon wood drivers of the day. Bobby Jones, after watching Nicklaus overpower the field to win the 1965 Masters, uttered his famous quote: "He played a game with which I am not familiar.

FIDDLER ON FLIGHT

On Saturday, February 5, 2011, I was in Columbus, Ohio, to call an Oilers-Blue Jackets game for CBC. Most people (especially hockey fans) assume that working for Hockey Night in Canada is a glamorous endeavour and, for the most part, they're right. You get the best seats in the best arenas to watch (and meet) the best hockey players on the planet – and you get paid for it. It all becomes decidedly unglamorous, however, when it comes time to travel. For this trip, I was up the morning after the game at 5:00 a.m. Eastern time to begin the arduous trek home. If you've ever traveled to or from Charlottetown in the dead of winter, you know that the routes are seldom direct and the connections are seldom timely. To put it charitably, it can be a bit of a challenge. My trip that day was a perfect example.

A 6:30 a.m. flight from Columbus landed in Chicago an hour later at 6:30 a.m. (seems like a typo, but remember: Chicago is in the Central Time Zone, an hour behind Columbus, which is in the Eastern Time Zone). A 7:30 a.m. flight from Chicago landed in Toronto at 10:15 a.m. (the flight is about 75 minutes, but Toronto is an hour ahead of Chicago). After clearing customs, I was told that my noon flight to Montreal was canceled and that I would consequently miss my 2:30 p.m. connection from Montreal home to Charlottetown. Instead, I was put on a 5:00 p.m. flight to Montreal, and rebooked on the 9:30 p.m. connection to Prince Edward Island. Killing four hours at Toronto's Pearson Airport is not an easy task (thank goodness for laptops and Seinfeld DVDs), but I did it. Mercifully, the new flight to Montreal took off on time and landed at 6:00 p.m. Now quite bleary-eyed, I immediately headed straight to the Air Canada lounge, in search of a bowl of soup and a comfortable chair. If you're having trouble following the itinerary to this point, I completely understand. I am, too! So here's the bottom line – as I sipped chicken noodle broth at Trudeau Airport, I had been traveling for 12 hours, and still had about 5 hours to go before the marathon ended.

If you've ever been to the airport in Montreal, you know that the departure area for flights traveling to PEI is a healthy distance from the main terminal. You have to take a long escalator to the bowels of the building, jump on a moving sidewalk to traverse an extensive underground tunnel, then reascend by another escalator at the end of the hall. From there, you turn right to find your gate. I had just made this 90-degree move when I heard an instantly recognizable voice – it sounded a bit like a foghorn in the distance...

"Bruce!"

I looked to my left through the crowd...

"Bruce!" (slightly louder, foghorn getting closer...)

I looked straight ahead, still in vain...

"Bruce!" (volume near full level, foghorn rapidly approaching...)

I looked to my right and, at long last, saw him. Fred "The Fiddler" MacDonald was making a beeline toward me at a speed reminiscent of Ben Johnson, post–water bottle swig. Fiddler had been attending a wine-tasting event in California and my initial impression was he had enjoyed it THOROUGHLY. From this point forward, he was on me like scales on a flounder...

"Bruce, come have a seat."

No sooner had I settled into my chair when Fiddler took a deep breath and launched into one of his patented stream-of-consciousness rants (please note: the following takes about 30 seconds to read, but Fiddler was able to get it all out in the most frenetic 10 seconds of speech you've ever heard)...

"Bruce, did I ever tell you about Vern Handrahan? You might recall, though I doubt it because it's before your time, that he pitched with the Oakland A's in the 1960s. He learned to pitch in our back yard, 26 Spring Street in Charlottetown. My father, Fiddler, who is in the PEI Sports Hall of Fame, was a standout for Amherst St. Pats before Word War II and his catcher Bill Kiley, who played in the major leagues as a catcher with the St. Louis Browns organization, wrote me and told me that Dad was the best pitcher he ever caught. Anyway, Dad built a pitching mound in our back yard, and showed Vern some of the finer points about pitching, how to grip the ball, make it rise, make it sink, how to hold hitters on base, etc. Vern went from there, pitched with senior teams in Charlottetown, then to the Halifax and District semi-pro league before moving into the pro ranks. Vern pitched and played with guys like Reggie Jackson, Joe Rudi, Sal Bando, and Vida Blue. He's the only Islander that ever played in the major leagues in the modern era. What do you think about that?"

Stunned and exhausted, I could only muster a single "Wow."

Undeterred, Fiddler reloaded and unleashed again...

"Here's another baseball story: Did you ever hear about Don "Duck" MacLeod, born and raised in Charlottetown with two other brothers, all top athletes. All graduates of Boston College..."

Have you ever been in a situation like this, where someone is talking so much and so quickly that you nod your head reflexively but, truth be told, you aren't really processing a thing? That's the state I rapidly reached with Fiddler. He kept talking, but I started hearing like this...

"He was an outstanding pitcher and was one of the final cuts of the Milwaukee Braves blah, blee, blue..."

(Head nodding...)

"I could play a bit, too, you know. Give me a minute here to tell you tozzin teezin true..."

(Head nodding, eyelids getting heavy...)

"Let me tell you about a horse called 'The Big Fred.' I breed a few mares at my place at Kingston, PEI, just a stone's throw from Charlottetown fleezing flobbin flue..."

By now, I was barely conscious, but had somehow found a comfortable rapport with Fiddler. He would talk, I would nod. A quick breath, and then rinse-repeat. But suddenly, like a lightning bolt out of the blue, massive trouble for me...

"Bruce, I was just wondering, breezing blobbin brookkie?"

The rise in his voice at the end of his sentence indicated that Fiddler had just asked me a question. And even though I was looking straight at him and nodding, I had no idea what it was. At this point, I had two options: 1) be truthful and admit that I hadn't been paying full attention, or 2) try to bluff my way out of this. Fancying myself a professional broadcaster and aspiring wordsmith, I decided to go for the prize behind door number two.

"Fiddler," I said, "That's such an interesting way of phrasing that question. Perhaps, however, if you were to put it in a slightly different context, it would afford me the opportunity to give you an answer slightly broader in scope."

Looking slightly bewildered, Fiddler nonetheless granted my wish...

"Fine, Bruce, I'll rephrase it. What is the age of your brother?"

Damn, should have gone with door number one!

This would be an ideal place for this story to conclude, but it gets even better. Just moments after the "How old is your brother?" debacle, we were asked to board the plane. I innocently and politely asked Fiddler where he was sitting. He said, "2A, window, how about you?" Glancing down at my boarding pass for the first time, I read with sheer terror, "2C, aisle, RIGHT BESIDE YOU!!"

The instant we boarded and were seated, it began again...

"On the topic of fastball, did you know that my brothers Tex, Sock, and Sput all were all named All-Canadian during the 1970s and 80s, when the game was at its peak of popularity..."

Only this time, he started scratching his elbow.

"Tex in left field, Sock at shortstop, and Sput as a catcher..."

(More elbow scratching...)

"They are the three of the best players ever to play the game in the Maritimes..."

(Working hard now on the elbow...)

I finally interrupt and ask, "What the heck is wrong with you?"

Fiddler says, "Oh, nothing to worry about. It's just my piles acting up again."

At that moment, what I always suspected was conclusively confirmed...

This guy doesn't know his arse from his elbow!

(Okay, okay...the last part of that story is total fiction. All, that is, except for the punch line!)

Favourite Trivia Question #5

Name the only player to be a Boston Celtic teammate of both Bill Russell and Larry Bird.

BOOMER – *POISSON ET FRITES*

In January of 2005, the best Canadian Junior Hockey team ever assembled easily won the World Junior Championship, played that year in Grand Forks, North Dakota. Team Canada was loaded with talent – Shea Weber, Dion Phaneuf, Brent Seabrook, Braydon Coburn on defence, and Patrice Bergeron, Jeff Carter, Ryan Getzlaf, Corey Perry, Mike Richards, and seventeen-year-old Sidney Crosby up front.

It was around that time I realized that Sidney was, in all likelihood, playing his last year of major junior hockey. He was the odds-on favourite to go number one in that year's draft, and it was inconceivable he would start the next hockey season anywhere but in the NHL. So, with this in mind, I came up with a little plan.

That year, I had a large build-up of Air Canada Aeroplan points. Enough, in fact, to easily fly four people round trip from Charlottetown to Rimouski, where Sidney played for the Oceanic. It dawned on me that a dual father-and-son trip might be a blast, so I asked Boomer if he and his son, Brad, would like to join my father, Mark, and me. He quickly said yes, especially after discovering that the flight was on me.

Now I'm not saying Boomer's cheap, but I reckon he'd have to hire a private detective just to find his wallet. This is a guy who hates to even tip his hat!

We chose the weekend of March 10–12, 2005, for our trip. We landed in Mont Joli, Quebec, on Friday mid-morning, rented a car, and made a 30-kilometre beeline for the Rimouski Coliseum. We arrived just in time to catch the end of the Oceanic morning skate and have a quick chat with Sidney. He asked us where we would be sitting at the games that weekend. It was a question that, at the time, seemed innocent. But the answer was one Sidney clearly filed away.

Rimouski is a lovely little town on the St. Lawrence River, in the Gaspé region of Quebec. It is predominantly French. Boomer, despite the last name "Gallant," isn't. This became apparent the first time we sat down for lunch, and he had to point at the menu in order to convey his choice to the waitress. This clearly bothered Boomer because a) he loves to talk and b) he thinks he's charming. So, at that moment, he vowed that by the end of the weekend he would actually order a meal in the native language of the region. No more menu-pointing, no more shortcuts. On top of that, he guaranteed that when the day of reckoning arrived, his dialect and elocution would be impeccable, and that any server would only assume French was his first language.

I, for one, was certainly intrigued by his bravado. Playing along, I suggested to him that he should begin preparing immediately, and asked what he was likely to order as his last meal of the trip. Without hesitation he answered, "Fish and chips."

"That's easy," I responded. "That's *'poisson et frites.'*"

"Say that again..."

"*Poisson et frites.*"

"*Poisson et frites?*"

"That's it."

"*Poisson et frites?*"

"Yes, you've got it."

"*Poisson et frites?*"

And so it continued – Boomer practicing, me confirming. Over and over and over for the rest of the day.

Back to hockey. That night, Rimouski played Rouyn-Noranda and won the game 10-6. Sidney had three goals and four assists in a tour de force performance. After each goal, guess where he glanced and pointed ever so subtly? Right at us, seated exactly where we told him earlier that day. Very cool...

Anyway, a long day eventually ends and we all retire for the night, the Gallants to their room and the Rainnies to ours. Just as Dad and I are about to doze off, the phone rings and startles us from our half-sleep. I answer and hear...

"*Poisson et frites?*"

"Go to bed."

The next morning, waiting in the lobby, the clerk at the front desk calls me over. "A call for you, Mr. Rainnie," he says.

"Hello," I say.

"*Poisson et frites?*"

I hang up, wishing now I had never even remotely encouraged this.

The Oceanic take to the ice that day for an afternoon game, this one versus Val d'Or. Once more Sidney dominates, scoring 3 goals and 2 assists as his team wins 8-4. Again with each goal, he points in our direction. But this time, a new wrinkle – as the crowd stands and chants, "Sidney, Sidney, Sidney," one lone spectator is bellowing in unison, "*Poisson et frites, poisson et frites!*" I pretend not to know him.

This unforgettable trip comes to an end the next day, but not before Boomer's newfound bilingualism is put to the ultimate test. Prior to leaving for the airport, we return to the diner where it all began. The moment of truth has arrived. As fate would have it, the very same waitress is serving our table. Boomer pretends to study the menu intently, as if he's not exactly sure what he might order. When his turn comes around, he hesitates, again giving the impression that the decision is excruciating...

"Monsieur?"

Boomer frowns and winces, as though this choice is now actually causing him physical discomfort.

"Monsieur?"

"*Oui*," he finally answers ("*Oui*," by the way, is the other word he has mastered during this excursion). With continued feigned reluctance and at long last, he makes his pick...

"*Poisson and frites*." He utters it flawlessly.

The waitress, visibly impressed with his inflection and intonation, smiles and cheerfully responds with, "*Oui, monsieur!*"

And then, just as she begins to walk away, Boomer stops her dead in her tracks as he blurts out at full volume, "Hey, I forgot – DO YOU HAVE ANY COLESLAW???"

Talk about blowing your cover! That's my Boomer – smooth as grade 9 sandpaper!

DREAM INTERVIEWS

The following are people I've never interviewed, but would love to. Hey, a guy can dream, can't he?

Paul Simon

He's one of my two great musical heroes and appeals to me on so many levels. He's a remarkable acoustic guitar player, a man with a strong social conscience (he devotes countless hours and dollars to making life a little better for homeless children in the US), a lifelong fan of the New York Yankees, the creative force behind my favourite album of all-time (*Graceland*), and the author of some of the most enduring songs of the past half-century. Strip away the melodies and his best songs ("The Boxer," "Bridge Over Troubled Water," "Graceland," "Still Crazy After All These Years," "Hearts and Bones," "America," "American Tune") stand alone as pre-eminent pieces of poetry. Hemingway once said, "To be great, you have to last." Paul Simon was a major cultural figure in the 1960s, and he remains one in 2011. That's six decades of relevance. And he shows no signs of stopping.

Julie Payette

I've always been captivated by all things NASA, and Julie Payette in particular has always fascinated me. Here's a Canadian woman who has completed two space flights and took part in the assembly of the International Space Station. Beyond that, though, here's someone who's an accomplished skier, scuba diver, and tennis player. She has a commercial pilot license with a float rating (meaning she can land on and take off from water). She's fluent in French, English, Spanish, Italian, Russian, and German. Plus, she plays piano and sang with the Montreal Symphony Orchestra.

And if that's not enough, she has a clever sense of culture and history. Among the items she's taken into space: a Lennie Gallant CD and a signed Maurice "The Rocket" Richard jersey.

Barack Obama

I'd love to sit across from him and, no matter the topic, just enjoy the rhythm of his speech. I'm not sure that we've seen a greater orator in the last half-century.

Martina Navratilova

She's one of the three greatest female tennis players ever, a cancer survivor, a gay rights advocate, and a defector from the country formerly known as Czechoslovakia – think we could find something to talk about?

David Letterman

He can vacillate from being so eloquently insightful to being hysterically funny, sometimes in the same sentence. There will never be another Johnny Carson, but Letterman is at least in the ballpark.

Clint Eastwood

My all-time favourite actor has had a remarkable run. Perhaps the most noteworthy aspect of his career is this: his very best work as an actor or director (*Unforgiven, In the Line of Fire, The Bridges of Madison County, Mystic River, Million Dollar Baby, Gran Torino*) has come AFTER the age of 60. Here's a guy who'd clearly rather wear out than rust out. I'd love to see if he'd share his longevity secrets.

Rachel Robinson

She is the wife of the late Jackie Robinson, the first black man to play major league baseball. I think we can only imagine what he had to go through – the daily battles to maintain his sanity, essence, and honour. I'd love to hear from her what it was like, and how she helped him through it.

Tiger Woods

Can you imagine the possibilities if no questions were off-limits? Further imagine the possibilities if there was no time limit.

Jim Balsillie

His is the story of a rise and fall. Here's a Canadian visionary who oversaw the development of the Blackberry, became a billionaire along the way, and then watched his company slowly be overtaken by Apple and the iPad. He has also been repeatedly thwarted in his attempts to purchase an NHL franchise. Outspoken and intense, he would be a dream interview subject.

Bruce Springsteen

This is my other musical hero, and all-time favourite singer-songwriter and performer. As with Paul Simon, the lyrics to his best songs ("Thunder Road," "Born to Run," "The Promised Land," "The River," "Nebraska," "The Rising") are by themselves sublime works of poetry.

In his classic song, "Racing in the Street," Springsteen suggests that you have two choices in life. One is to give up living, and slowly fade away. The other is to come home, wash up, and go out and do something.

Springsteen has clearly chosen the latter option. You simply can't be that prolific for that long without being tireless and dedicated. He's always emptied his tank, and I hope he does so for many more albums and tours to come.

FOR ARGUMENT'S SAKE...

The following is intended strictly for sports fans and is included solely for the purpose of provoking debate. In other words, I'm looking to get you a little riled up! So read away, and be sure to let me know where you think I'm spot-on and, conversely, where you think I need to give my head a shake...

The lists that follow are made up solely of players I have seen "live," either on television or in person.

NHL ALL-TIME TEAMS
(First Team)

Goalie – Patrick Roy

Won two Stanley Cups in Montreal basically by himself, and added two more for good measure with better teams in Colorado.

Defence – Bobby Orr

Bobby Clarke, who was frugal with his compliments, once mused, "There's stars, there's superstars, and then there's Bobby Orr." Enough said...

Defence – Nicklas Lidström

After six Norris trophies for best defenceman and after four Stanley Cups, you can make a solid argument that Lidström is the second-best defenceman ever to play the game.

A couple of years back, when Sidney Crosby was home for the summer, I asked him this question: "Who is the one player you knew was great, but until you actually played against him, didn't know how great?"

Sidney didn't hesitate for a second. "Lidström," he said. "He's so smart, and might just be the best passer in the NHL."

Pretty good endorsement, don't you think?

Centre – Mario Lemieux

I think that when fully healthy, Mario was just slightly more dominant than Wayne Gretzky. With his strength and reach, he could totally take over a game.

Right Wing – Guy Lafleur

He was the first player ever to record six straight 50-goal, 100-point seasons. He was also exceptional in the clutch.

Left Wing – Bobby Hull

I only really saw "The Golden Jet" from 1974 on. He was slightly past his prime by then, but still enough of a force to play a pivotal role for Team Canada in both the '74 series versus Russia and the 1976 Canada Cup. I've always believed that if Orr and Hull had played for Team Canada in 1972, the series with the Soviet Union would not have been nearly as close.

Coach – Scotty Bowman

He is likely the best coach ever in any sport.

(Second Team)

Goalie – Bernie Parent

Some of my earliest hockey-watching memories are of Bernie Parent almost single-handedly leading the Philadelphia Flyers to two straight Stanley Cups. In Philadelphia to this day, you can still purchase a bumper sticker that reads, "Only God saves more than Bernie!"

Defence – Denis Potvin

He was the captain of the New York Islanders team that won four straight Stanley Cups to start the 1980s. As a defenceman, he had it all: strong as an ox, durable, superb wristshot, and passes that were always on the money.

Defence – Ray Bourque

No defenceman ever scored more career points than Ray Bourque.

Centre – Wayne Gretzky

Holder of 61 NHL records. Enough said...

Right Wing – Mike Bossy

He might score 100 goals with Gretzky as his centre. The most natural, pure goal scorer I've ever seen.

Right Wing – Bob Gainey

Here I'll go with the best defensive forward in the history of hockey. After all, with Gretzky and Bossy on this line, someone would need to backcheck!

Coach – Al Arbour

He had the good fortune of being named coach of the New York Islanders the same year that Denis Potvin arrived on the scene. Together, they built a Long Island dynasty.

MLB ALL-TIME TEAM

Right-Handed Pitcher – Pedro Martinez

You could argue that for a four-year stretch (1997 with Montreal, 1998–2000 with Boston), no right-hander was ever better.

Left-Handed Pitcher – Randy Johnson

He blossomed at age twenty-nine, and for the next ten years, like Koufax in his prime, was a threat to throw a no-hitter every single time he started a game...

Reliever – Mariano Rivera

Here's the telltale sign of how truly great he is – for the past fifteen years, it's been a front page sports headline when he's actually blown a save. And his postseason numbers are incomparable – over the course of 31 series (divisional, league, and World), he's posted a record of 8 and 1, with 42 saves and an ERA of 0.71. Safe to say, he'd be the reliever on any "All-Time" team.

Catcher – Johnny Bench

Probably the greatest catcher ever to play the game... Wonderful in the clutch, peerless throwing arm, superb hitter, uncanny handler of pitchers...

In a book called *The Machine*, by the great baseball writer Joe Posnanski, there's a wonderful story involving Bench and a pitcher named Gerry Arrigo. Bench was a rookie, and Arrigo was pitching one day against the Dodgers. His fastball had very little zip to begin with, and on this day it was slower than usual. Bench kept calling for the curve. Arrigo kept shaking him off. Finally, Bench went to the mound and said something to the effect of, "Your fastball stinks, throw the bleeping curve." Arrigo told him to keep quiet and get back behind the plate. Bench paused, turned, and walked slowly away. Crouching behind homeplate, he called for the curve. Arrigo shook his head. He called again for the curve. Arrigo again defiantly shook him off. Exasperated, Bench called for the fastball. Arrigo threw, and Bench reached out with his bare right hand and caught it! "Now throw the bleeping curve!" Bench yelled, as he blistered the ball back to his pitcher.

First Baseman – Albert Pujols

In 2010, he batted .312 and led the National League with 42 home runs, 118 RBIs, and 115 runs scored. And for Pujols, this wasn't even a good year!

Second Baseman – Joe Morgan

He was the little guy who made the Big Red Machine go! The Reds won the World Series in 1975 and 1976. Guess who was named National League MVP both seasons?

Shortstop – Cal Ripken Jr.

It's the toughest call on this team, but I'm choosing a two-time

American League MVP and the only shortstop currently in the 3,000-hit, 400-home run club. Plus, you know he's never going to miss a game.

Third Base – Mike Schmidt

Along with Bench and Rivera, this guy is another undeniable member of the "All-Time" team. Three-time MVP, 12-time All-Star, 10-time Gold Glove winner, 1980 World Series MVP, and 8 times led the National League in home runs.

Left Field – Carl Yastrzemski

"Yaz" was a remarkable defensive left-fielder and especially so in Fenway Park, where he was a master at playing tricky caroms off the Green Monster. And, at the plate, few hitters in history were ever better in pressure situations. Barry Bonds was a marvel (even prior to his late-career chemical enhancement) and Rickey Henderson a supreme athlete, but neither could match Yastrzemski when it came to heart and love for the game.

Centre Field – Ken Griffey Jr.

The single greatest baseball talent of my lifetime – watching Griffey Jr. in Seattle is what watching Willie Mays must have been like.

Right Field – Ichiro Suzuki

Batting leadoff for my team will be a man who has led the Major Leagues in hits seven times! He is also baseball's best defensive right fielder, with tremendous range and a cannon for an arm.

Manager – Joe Torre

He lasted 12 full seasons in New York with George Steinbrenner, leading the Yankees to four World Series. Have you ever heard a player, current or former, say anything bad about him?

NBA ALL-TIME TEAMS
(First Team)

Point Guard – Magic Johnson

No-brainer. He's the one guy who instantly made each of his four teammates on the court exponentially better players. For that reason alone, I think he's in the discussion for "Greatest Player of All-Time." The next guy probably wins that one, though...

Shooting Guard – Michael Jordan

No-brainer. Arguably the best offensive AND defensive player ever!

Small Forward – Larry Bird

Third straight no-brainer. Best passing forward ever, and, man, could he shoot! My favourite Larry Bird story comes from the 1988 All-Star Weekend in Chicago. On that Saturday night, Bird was taking part in the three-point shooting contest. He had won the event the previous two years, and was looking for the "three-peat." Before the shootout began, Bird strode into the locker room and casually asked, "Who's finishing second?" It came down to the last ball. Bird fired, and a split-second later, with the ball barely off his fingers, turned and walked away with his index finger in the air. The ball, of course, went in.

Years later, an interviewer asked Larry Bird about this moment, and suggested the comment and subsequent gesture were a bit cocky. Bird's response: "It ain't bragging if you can back it up!"

Power Forward – Tim Duncan

Yet another no-brainer. Along with Stan Musial, in my opinion the most underrated sports superstar of all-time. Four-time NBA champion...

Centre – Shaquille O'Neal

Could have gone with Kareem, but Shaq's three-year run with the Lakers, from 2000 to 2002, sways me in his direction. Three straight championships, three straight Finals MVP awards...

Coach - Phil Jackson

No coach has ever handled superstars better.

(Second Team)

Point Guard – Isiah Thomas

Not the easiest guy to like, but impossible not to admire. Captain of back-to-back NBA title teams in 1989 and 1990, he just might be the best "little man" ever to play the game.

Shooting Guard – Kobe Bryant

Next to Jordan, the fiercest competitor I've ever seen on a basketball court.

Small Forward – Lebron James

Along with Wilt Chamberlain, arguably the greatest athlete ever to play in the NBA...6'8", 270 pounds of pure muscle, and lightning fast. One or two times EVERY game, he does something that you swear you've never seen before.

Power Forward – Kevin McHale

Karl Malone, Charles Barkley, and Kevin Garnett were all magnificent, but none were as unstoppable near the basket as Kevin McHale of the Boston Celtics. His endless array of low-post moves made him virtually impossible to defend. I was a diehard Laker fan in the 1980s and McHale terrified me just as much as Larry Bird. Seriously, that's how good he was...

Centre – Kareem Abdul-Jabbar

A model of longevity and consistency, his skyhook was equal parts beautiful and unstoppable. Here's the most amazing fact about Jabbar: he was named NBA Finals MVP in 1971 with the Milwaukee Bucks, and again in 1985 with the Los Angeles Lakers. Basketball fans, that's a span of fourteen years! Remarkable...

Coach - Pat Riley

He led the Lakers to four titles in the 1980s, and then won another in 2006 as coach of the Miami Heat.

TENNIS GREATS
Best Male Players I've Seen

1) Roger Federer

The most graceful athlete I've ever seen in any sport... Winner of 16 career Grand Slam titles.

2) Pete Sampras

Possessed the best serve, overhead, and arguably forehand of any male player ever to play the game... Winner of 14 career Grand Slam titles.

3) Rafael Nadal

Perhaps the strongest, most determined athlete in professional sports today... Winner of 9 Grand Slam titles (and counting), plus an Olympic Gold Medal.

4) Bjorn Borg

Had a marvelous, penetrating topspin forehand, an underrated backhand and serve, and footspeed that was unmatched in his era... Winner of 11 Grand Slams (6 French Opens, 5 consecutive Wimbledons)...

5) John McEnroe

Tracy Austin, who won two US Opens, told me that McEnroe had the greatest hands and most natural talent of any player she ever saw... Winner of 7 Grand Slam titles.

Best Female Players I've Seen

1) Martina Navratilova

Winner of 18 Grand Slam singles titles, 31 Grand Slam doubles titles, and 10 Grand Slam mixed doubles titles... Her 1983 season might have been the most dominant in tennis history: 86 wins and just 1 loss (to little-known American Kathy Horvath in the 4th round at the French Open).

2) Steffi Graf

Winner of 22 Grand Slam singles titles... Many would give her the nod over Navratilova, but I can't for two reasons... 1) She was nowhere near as masterful at the net, and therefore nowhere near as skilled a doubles player, and 2) her Grand Slam numbers would be not nearly as extraordinary had Monica Seles not been stabbed in 1993 (Seles was by far the top female player in the game at the time).

3) Serena Williams

Winner of 13 Grand Slam singles titles, 12 Grand Slam doubles titles, and 2 Grand Slam mixed doubles titles... Her serve, forehand, and volley are great, and her two-handed backhand is off the charts.

4) Monica Seles

Winner of 9 Grand Slam singles titles... When she was stabbed in April of 1993, she had won 7 of the last 8 Grand Slams she had played, and had beaten Steffi Graf in 3 of their 4 Grand Slam finals.

5) Chris Evert

Winner of 18 Grand Slam singles titles, including a record 7 at the French Open and a record 6 at the US Open... In terms of athleticism and strength, however, just not quite in the same league as the women who precede her on this list... She once opined of her great rival Navratilova, "Her best was better than my best, and that hurts me to say."

A COUPLE OF MISFITS

"It is a privilege to be calling this sport in the era of Eric Lamaze and Hickstead. How many Canadian athletes can say they are without peer, unequivocally the best in the world? Together, Lamaze and Hickstead can. And today is just further proof."

Those were the exact words I chose on September 11 of 2011. I used them to conclude CBC's broadcast of the CN International, one of the most prestigious show jumping events in the world, held annually at Spruce Meadows in Calgary, Alberta. On a magnificent, sun-drenched afternoon at what is, without doubt, the premier sporting venue in the country (sorry, Bell Centre in Montreal and Air Canada Centre in Toronto, but you're not even close), Canada's greatest-ever sporting duo were at their very peak. Forty thousand fans were there in person to watch the flawless performance of Lamaze and his stallion. Hundreds of thousands more were glued to the edges of seats all across the country. What none of us knew, though, and what none of us even remotely suspected, was that we were witnessing the final magnificent moment for this legendary partnership.

Fast forward just two months, to November 6 of 2011. I was in Sault Ste. Marie, Ontario, calling the final of the World Cup of Curling. During the 4th end of the game, I noticed the red light on my Blackberry blinking. After we had gone to commercial, I checked for the message. It was from a favourite CBC Sports producer by the name of Jeff Pearlman. Knowing he was watching the curling broadcast, I opened it expecting to find some constructive criticism, or something funny and light. What I found instead was instantly and totally devastating. Jeff's message contained the news that Hickstead had passed away suddenly from a massive heart attack at a competition in Verona, Italy. Could this really be true? I wondered how it was even possible. He was only sixteen years old – still fairly young in the equine world – and I had just seen him at the peak of his powers only weeks earlier. My mind began to race, and it flashed back to the time when Lamaze was more outcast than superstar, and when Hickstead was the horse that nobody wanted.

So many people view show jumping as an elitist sport, a playground for bluebloods. In many cases, that is true. But Eric Lamaze was the antithesis to that line of thinking. He was born to a drug-addicted mother. He barely knew his father, who was absent far more than present. He quit school in grade 8 and was raised on a farm by an alcoholic grandmother. It was here, though, he discovered the thing that would come to define him: he loved horses.

In 2004, his career was at a bit of a crossroads. Sure he had talent and yes he would win the occasional event. But he was a healthy distance from "Number One Rider in the World" billing. In fact, he was best known not for his potential or ability, but for being banned from the 1996 and 2000 Olympics after testing positive for cocaine. It was against this backdrop that he made a trip to Belgium to search for a partner that might take him to the next level. At the very end of a long day of viewing, Lamaze was introduced to Hickstead. The horse was far from physically impressive. He was actually smaller than average, standing only 16 hands high (a hand is equal to 4 inches; by comparison, Canada's other great jumper, "Big Ben," stood over 17 hands high). Still, Lamaze was attracted by the horse's smooth lines and slim physique and decided to give him a try. To say they immediately hit it off would be grand overstatement. In fact, Lamaze could barely even get on him; the horse was rebellious and hot-tempered. But once he did, he sensed there might be something good there, that he might be able to channel the stallion's reckless power. He bought him. And the rest is a story of a horse becoming a rider's redemption.

Forever, the sport of show jumping had been dominated by Europeans and, to a lesser extent, Americans. But Lamaze and Hickstead were the exception, the unbeatable Canadian connection. In their seven years together they made magic, winning close to $4 million, countless grand prix titles, World Championship medals, and, most memorably, two Olympic Medals in Beijing.

Hickstead was not an imposing stallion, but he seemed to know that knocking fences down was a bad thing, and he worked his ass off to get over them. He had that rare champion's ability to stretch his body to clear a rail or lean back just enough to hit a jump at just the right angle. Most important, he had a pilot who let him be who he was. Perhaps just as important, Hickstead let his pilot be who he was, too. I remember once speaking to Lamaze, who summed up the relationship succinctly.

"We grew together, and we kind of became one personality," Eric said. "We're both short, we're not graceful, we're pretty nervy, and just hate to lose. When I look into his eyes, I see so much of myself..."

It was Lamaze's plan to take Hickstead to the 2012 Olympics in London, where he would have been heavily favoured to repeat as individual show jumping gold medalist. He would then let Hickstead retire and enjoy a life of well-deserved luxury. Alas, it was not be. Fate had a more sudden and tragic denouement in mind.

If you haven't seen the video from Verona, consider yourself lucky – it is just so terribly sad. As hard as it is to watch, though, it is telling. Hickstead, on a day when he was near death, carried Lamaze through a near flawless round, and cleared the last rail with ease. As he left the ring, his legs buckled, his huge heart literally bursting. But as he fell backward, he still managed to protect his partner, setting Lamaze down gently and allowing him to dismount unharmed. The exact final moment is both heartbreaking and poignant – the horse giving one last look to his rider, just to make sure that everything was OK.

A loyal friend to the very end. The partner of a lifetime. And solid proof of what can happen if someone just believes in you.

Favourite Trivia Question #6

The most consistent and most underrated of baseball's all-time greats finished his career with the identical number of hits at home as on the road. Who is he?

MY FAVOURITE INTERVIEW

I get asked quite often, "What's the favourite interview you've ever done?"

Now, this might sound like a tough one, but, for me, it's a no-brainer. In fact, this is the easiest question in the world for me to answer, ranking just slightly ahead of, "What year was the War of 1812?" and "Does Boomer Gallant ever pay for lunch?" For the official response, let me take you back to Thursday, November 14 of the year 2000...

I was working in Halifax at the time, co-hosting the CBC supper-hour news for Nova Scotia. My partner then was a wonderful statuesque woman by the name of Linda Kelly (maybe the single kindest, most genuine person I've ever met in this business). The show was set up in such a way that Linda would host from the studio, and I would do several live "hits" from a remote location. So, it became my job every day to find a place where something interesting and television-friendly was happening.

On this particular Thursday I had planned to broadcast from a local gymnastics academy where a group of athletes were in training for an upcoming competition. At around 11 o'clock that morning, I received a call saying that the coach was a bit under the weather and that the plans would have to be postponed. Needing to come up quickly with an alternative, I opened *The Chronicle Herald* newspaper and hastily turned to the entertainment section. It was there I saw an article that talked about a fiddler from Antigonish who had a new CD called *Over the Waves*. As I read further, I discovered that she was officially releasing this CD that very night at a Halifax establishment called The Old Triangle Alehouse. Thinking that this had the potential for a lively segment in the program, I called the number provided at the end of the article, and was a tad surprised when the fiddler herself answered...

"Hi, this is Kendra MacGillivray," came the voice.

"Hi, Kendra, my name is Bruce Rainnie, and I work for CBC TV. I have something I'd like to run by you if you have a minute."

"Sure," she said. "Go right ahead."

"Well, I was wondering if we could do a couple of live drop-ins tonight during your CD release at the Old Triangle. You know, you could play a couple of tunes with your band, and then we could talk a bit about your new CD..."

"That would be great!" she replied, with little hesitation. "What time do we need to be ready?"

"Well, if you're all set to go by 6:15 or so, that would work out well."

"No problem," she said. "We'll be there. I look forward to meeting you."

"Same here," I replied. "See you tonight."

With that, I breathed a sigh of relief, knowing that my guest for the evening was booked and that she would no doubt inject some much-appreciated energy into our program. There was one slight problem, though – I knew absolutely NOTHING about her. So, I spent the next few hours with my good friend "Google," learning all I could about Kendra, the fiddle, and Celtic music in general.

Armed confidently with my newfound knowledge of jigs and reels, I arrived at the Old Triangle about a half-hour or so before we were set to go to air. To my astonishment, the place was already pretty much packed. Every seat at every table was taken, and the standing-room area was essentially shoulder to shoulder. I jostled my way to a spot near the stage in the far corner of the room, wondering frankly what all the fuss could be about. My curiosity was emphatically satisfied mere moments later when I gazed toward the front door, and saw Kendra walk through...

It's an entrance that's forever etched in my memory. In she strode, sporting a pair of tantalizing, formfitting black leather pants, her curly strawberry-blond hair pulled back in a pony tail, her huge, dazzling, almost indescribably pale blue eyes scanning the room. She was absolutely stunning and radiant. Suffice to say, my gast was totally flabbered! (Let me check for a moment to see if I mentioned the black leather pants. Oh, yes, it was just a sentence ago...)

As she approached the stage and her eyes met mine, it took every ounce of focus I could muster to actually remember my name and introduce myself in some sort of manner approaching professional. She thanked me for coming, took her fiddle from her case, and began the process of making sure it was in tune. As I watched her (trying desperately hard not to ogle), I remember thinking, "Okay, I've had a really fulfilling day. One of my best days ever, actually. From here on, everything else is just a bonus." And as if on cue, Kendra and her band kicked in...

They absolutely blew the roof off the place with a ten-minute set that featured some of the finest musicianship I had ever seen close up. The room was just buzzing, totally electric really. As the set came to a rousing conclusion, I moved in for the interview. Mesmerized again by her eyes (and, yes, the damn pants), I stumbled my way through three or four questions, and then got the heck out of the way so she could play some more music. When she finished, and the roar from the crowd had settled, I approached her to say a quick "goodbye" before she launched into another tune...

"This was a blast," I said. "It was great to meet you and hear you play. Thanks so much for being on the show."

"No, thank you," she replied. "It was really nice to meet you, too."

"Maybe I'll see you again sometime soon," I offered hopefully.

And then, the four words that filled me with a mix of wonder and hope...

"That would be nice," she said.

And here is where fate took one look at me, had pity, and decided it was time to get involved. As the music resumed, and I turned to walk away from the stage, the very first person I bumped into was my favourite CBC cameraman, Eric Woolliscroft. He wasn't working, but was instead enjoying a night out with his wife, Lynn.

"What are you doing here?" I asked him.

"Just here supporting Kendra, that's all," he answered.

"You know her?"

"Yes, pretty well."

"How?"

"I shot a feature with her a few months back. She's great, isn't she?"

"Yeah, she sure seems to be. Well, see you tomorrow at work."

"OK, see ya."

The next day, the very second Eric arrived, I sprinted to his desk at a speed that would have made Usain Bolt stand up and take notice...

"Listen, you have to do me a big favour," I said, trying to catch my breath.

"Sure, what is it?"

"Well, you said you know Kendra?"

"Yes."

"Look, you have to find out if she has some clown in her life."

"What do you mean by 'clown'?"

"You know, some idiot!"

(In retrospect, I find it quite entertaining that I was already angry and clearly jealous over some guy I wasn't sure even existed...)

"I don't think she's going out with anyone."

"Well, can you find out for certain?"

"No problem – I'll send her an e-mail right now and ask her."

"OK, cool."

A couple of hours later, Eric marched proudly to my desk, and offered up the words that were music to my ears...

"She's single, buddy."

My clever reply: "YOU ARE THE MAN!"

Mere moments later, I was on the phone with Kendra, asking if we could get together to chat more about her music career (seriously – that was my line!). Thankfully, I clearly caught her in a charitable moment, because she accepted my invitation. A week or so later, I took her to dinner at The Press Gang restaurant in Halifax. We talked and talked for hours until we closed the place. We haven't stopped talking since...

So there you have it – by a landslide, my favourite interview. It was eleven years and two beautiful boys ago. Suffice to say, I loved her answers. And truth be told, she must have thought my questions were at least okay...

BOOMER – THE WEDDING TOAST

Kendra and I were married on December 29, 2004, at St. Ninian's Cathedral in Antigonish, Nova Scotia. Kendra was born in Antigonish and raised in Lanark, which is about ten minutes outside of the town. She had a definite vision of how she wanted the day to look and feel, and was able to realize it with elegant perfection. I was so proud of the way she brought everything and everyone together, and, as I write this now, I feel that pride welling up again.

My side of the wedding party that day featured six major players: my brother, Matt, as best man, and an eclectic collection of five groomsmen...

1) Lou LeBlanc

Lou is my broadcast mentor and longtime friend (you met him earlier in the "Broadcast Bug" chapter).

2) Al MacLean

Al is one of the premier television editors in the country. For the past seven years, he has worked hand in hand with Rick Mercer to help put together the highest-rated comedy program in Canada, "The Rick Mercer Report." I first met Al in 1995 at CBC in Halifax and we hit it off right away. My conservative guess is that he and I have played close to 250 rounds of golf together, each one funnier than the last.

3) John MacIntosh

John is one of my best friends from my time spent in Yarmouth. He's as good a bass player and harmony singer as you'll find anywhere. If I had a dollar for every hour spent in his basement playing tunes, I'd be in Bill Gates' tax bracket.

4) Mickey Fox

Mickey is likely the finest player ever to play university basketball in Canada. In the 1970s, he was a four-time All-Canadian and led Saint Mary's University to two national championships. He was also my idol. It's weird how life works because, years later, my idol became my buddy. Turns out he's an even better guy than he was a player...

5) Kevin "Boomer" Gallant

By now, you know plenty about him.

Not wanting to burden this esteemed group with tuxedo fittings and rentals over the Christmas holidays, I decided that the dress code for the wedding would be "business/informal." I wore my best black suit with a silver/black tie and matching pocket handkerchief. Five-sixths of my wedding attendants dressed with similar attention to detail. One-sixth clearly missed the memo...

Boomer showed up that day in a Johnny Carson tweed sports coat (circa 1978), black turtleneck, black Denver Hayes jeans, and the slickest pair of Wind River workboots you've ever seen (they had nice thick rubber soles that squeaked every time he took a step on the church floor). I shudder to think what he would have worn had I suggested "business/casual." (If you think I'm exaggerating, I urge you to look at the photo insert in this book. There you will see him, a majestic vision of unique sartorial splendour.)

Between the wedding and the reception, Boomer had time to doff his "suit" and change into his more customary Hawaiian shirt, shorts, and sandals. And given the way he was smiling like The Joker and walking slightly unevenly around the room, I also sensed he had found time to quench his thirst.

It was shortly after the toasts to the bride and groom that Lou, our emcee, uttered the words that sent a cold shiver down my spine...

"There's somebody special here tonight that would like to approach the head table and bring greetings from PEI. Ladies and gentlemen, a warm hand for everybody's favourite weatherman, BOOMER GALLANT!"

And there he was, haphazardly weaving his way through the crowd and making his way to the podium, with a look on his face so smug it reminded me of Simon Cowell about to offer a scathing review on "American Idol." Steadying himself behind the microphone, he took a cursory look at the assembled crowd and then, at typical Boomer decibel level, bellowed an opening line that a) instantly became one for the history books, and b) confirmed my suspicion that he was in fact at a significant level of lubrication...

"GOOD EVENING, PRINCE EDWARD ISLAND!!!"

This salutation was met fairly tepidly by our wedding guests. In fact, you could actually hear crickets chirping. And, no wonder, really, given that we were in a building located in the heart of northern Nova Scotia. Undeterred, Boomer pressed onward...

"Hey, great to see everybody here tonight. Hope you're all having a good time. And Bruce, nice suit! I guess it pays to be at the circus when the clown dies."

(This time, a bit of nervous laughter from the crowd.)

"Hey, folks, not sure if you heard, but a bit earlier today Bruce had to go to the doctor with a really bad earache. The doctor took one look at Bruce and said, 'Take off all your clothes, stand in front of the window, and do 10 jumping jacks.'

"Bruce said, 'But Doc, I just have an earache.' The doctor said, 'Yeah, I know, I'm just really ticked off at my neighbour.'"

(Laughter beginning to build...the sheer force of Boomer's personality beginning to win over the room...this wedding toast palpably morphing into a wedding roast...)

"Hey, folks, did you hear what happened yesterday. Bruce wanted to do something really special for Kendra on the day before their wedding, so he decided to take her for clams in Canso. They were driving along the highway when Bruce reached over and lovingly put his hand on Kendra's knee. Kendra looked down and then back up at Bruce and said, 'You know, we're almost married now, you can go a lot farther than that.'

"So Bruce drove to Cape Breton!"

(Big eruption, Gallant starting to roll...)

And then, in a room populated predominantly by conservative, elderly Catholics, Boomer pulled the ace from his sleeve. At that moment in time, he might have been the only person on the planet able to get away with what followed...

"And folks, as a special treat this evening, here is the forecast for Bruce and Kendra's honeymoon night, as issued by Environment Canada and Boomer...

"For tonight, a thunderstorm warning has been issued...

"A high pressure system will meet a warm front around midnight tonight, with heavy sounds of thumping and copious amounts of moisture.

"This storm will last two minutes as the high pressure fizzles, the warm front remains stationary, and temperatures remain hot and humid!

"Bangs of thunder will reoccur four hours later...however, this system is quick moving, as high pressure is blocked by a pillow!

"Tomorrow, skies will be sunny as precipitation dries up, with a 90 per cent chance of another thunderstorm tomorrow afternoon.

"Long-range outlook for Bruce and Kendra...nothing but clear skies and a bundle of sunshine, nine months from now!!"

That was almost six years ago, and, at last report, jaws are still being surgically removed from the floor of St. Ninian's Hall in Antigonish.

FATHERHOOD

At the Queen Elizabeth Hospital in Charlottetown, Unit 4 is where mothers and their newborn babies are sent to recover and bond after childbirth. When you, as a father, enter this unit, you walk down a hall and past a bank of windows on your left. After about fifteen steps or so, where the windows end, if you have the time to stop, I urge you to do so. Stop and look at the wall. There you'll find a framed etching, which features the following nugget...

"Life is not measured by the number of breaths we take, but by the moments that take our breath away."

Whoever chose this saying for this location knew exactly what they were doing. For, in life, there is nothing that leaves you wanting for air more than witnessing the birth of a child.

It leaves you breathless, but it also leaves you speechless, searching for words and searching for meaning. I have often heard little babies described as bundles of joy. They are certainly that. I've also heard them described as bundles of innocence. They are that, too. But, for me, neither characterization goes quite far enough or gets it quite right. For much of the past five years (since the birth of my oldest son), I've scoured the English language looking for that perfect word or concept. In a search that has proven mostly elusive, the best I've been able to come up with is "grace." Little babies are truly bundles of grace. And you as a parent recognize that instantly, at the moment of birth. You also instinctively grasp the essence of what it is to be a father or mother. Your job is to protect that grace and nurture it, until someday your child is secure enough to protect it on his/her own. By that time, you also hope they are ready to channel it in productive and benevolent ways.

Beyond that, though, I've always struggled to articulate just all that fatherhood means. I've always found the concepts of unconditional love, responsibility, and example-setting much too vast to succinctly put into words. That is, until March 28 of 2010, when I drove Murray McLauchlan around the streets of Charlottetown. I'm sure right now you're thinking, "What does the guy who wrote 'Farmer's Song' have to do with any of this?" Let me explain...

Murray was our musical guest at the 2010 Easter Seals Telethon. I was producer and co-host of this show, and had the pleasure of booking him to appear. He was great – generous, patient, enthusiastic – everything you could ever ask for in a marquee entertainer. After the broadcast, I invited Murray back to our home for a night of conversation and refreshments.

As we drove, the small talk drifted to parenthood. Murray has two children, a daughter, Sarah, who is nearing thirty, and a son, Duncan, who is in his late teens. When Murray finished detailing where his children were in their lives, I said something to the effect of, "There's nothing quite like being a Dad, is there?"

He smiled, looked out the passenger side window and then back to me, and responded with, "Well, you know, it takes four generations of Monarch butterflies to make it from Southern Ontario to Mexico."

I slowly nodded my head, trying to let on that I had some clue as to what he was talking about. And then, thankfully, after a moment's silence, he continued: "I learned that about Monarch butterflies in grade 8, and always thought that it would suck to be anything but that fourth generation! But then, when I had kids, I realized that the first three are meaningful, too."

What an unforgettable and so-easy-to-grasp metaphor for what fatherhood is all about. For when you look in the eyes of your child and let your mind and imagination run free, you realize you're just a link in a wonderful little genetic chain. You can see yourself, you can see your parents, and, if you look hard enough, you can even see your grandparents. But beyond that, and most importantly, you become instantly aware of what your primary role is as a Dad...

No matter the fears or obstacles you might encounter along the way, you have to do everything in your power to help your child get to his or her "Mexico." If you meet this goal, and even if this is your sole major accomplishment, then I would argue your life has been an overwhelming success.

This is one of my favourite pieces of poetry. It comes courtesy of my grade 11 Creative Writing teacher at Dartmouth High School in Nova Scotia. His name is Jim Falcone and he remains a friend to this day. Retired now, he was a sensational educator, and one of the most influential people I've encountered in my life. He encouraged expression and exploration, and, in my case, always found the good in stuff that was predominantly bad. I remember inundating him with a series of short stories I had written. All had plot twists I thought were clever, but, in retrospect, were as obvious as cows in a chicken coop. God love him, Jim always pretended to be surprised and entertained.

Anyway, back in 1984, he shared with me a poem he had written for his son. I loved it at the time and never really forgot it. When I asked Jim if I could use it in this book, he didn't hesitate for a moment. And when he sent it to me, it was better than I remembered. This is for any Dad who has a baby boy he's crazy about. Enjoy...

FATHER AND SON

Jim Falcone

We practiced all that afternoon
I'd pitch
you'd hit
sometimes miss
then laugh and laugh yourself
into a heap
on spring brown grass
your head-smile-eyes in clouds

For me
I enjoyed much more
the long ball gone above my aging leap
the thump of wood on sphere
that echoed future cheers
for you

The evening sun
behind your back
that night
and two home runs
upon your bat
I glowed and yelled
for more games won
and championships to come
while you
Antaeus unbound
just leaped into the air
never having rounded
third
before

Trivia Answers

1. Maurice "Rocket" Richard (played for Montreal and scored 50 in a season) and Henri Richard (played for Montreal); Phil Esposito (scored 50 in a season) and Tony Esposito (played for Montreal); Mickey Redmond (scored 50 and played for Montreal) and Dick Redmond; Marcel Dionne (scored 50) and Gilbert Dionne (played for Montreal); Pierre Turgeon (scored 50 and played for Montreal) and Sylvain Turgeon (also played for Montreal); Pavel Bure (scored 50) and Valeri Bure (played for Montreal).

2. Maurice Richard, Jean Beliveau, Stan Mikita, Gilbert Perreault, Mike Bossy, Mario Lemieux, Steve Yzerman, Jarome Iginla

3. Sonny Banks, Henry Cooper, and Joe Frazier

4. Teemu Selänne, Peter Stastny, Alex Ovechkin, Dale Hawerchuk, Sidney Crosby, Joe Juneau, Mario Lemieux

5. Don Chaney

6. Stan Musial (3,630 career hits: 1,815 at home, 1,815 on the road)